The Horticultural Handbook

*For the Guidance of Organisers,
Schedule-makers, Exhibitors
and Judges*

Revised 1990

The Royal Horticultural Society

Published by
The Royal Horticultural Society
80 Vincent Square, London SW1P 2PE

Copyright © The Royal Horticultural Society
1953, 1956, 1972, 1981, 1990
First published 1953
Fifth edition 1990

ISBN 0 906603 73 0

Cover photographs
Front: A display staged by Peper Harow at the Great Autumn
Show 1989, photographed by Photos GB
Back: RHS Ornamental Plant Competition
photographed by Michael Warren

Cartoons by David Thelwell

Typeset by A W Mailing Services Ltd, Ashford, Kent
Printed and bound by Spottiswoode Ballantyne, Colchester, Essex

CONTENTS

Show Stationery

The following items of show stationery are supplied by
RHS Enterprises Ltd, RHS Garden, Wisley, Woking,
Surrey GU23 6QB.
Prices and order form on application.

Entry-cards and prize labels
Cards for placing on competitive exhibits at shows (approx. 4¾
inches x 6 inches). They are white, printed in black, with a space
for the name of the society to be added locally.
Booklets are available for use with the cards, each containing
twelve gummed labels for 'First Prize', 'Second Prize', 'Third
Prize', and two blanks to be filled in as required. One booklet will
be sufficient for twelve classes.

Judges' Cards and Sheets
Ruled cards for judges' records of the prizewinners at shows, and
scoresheets for judging gardens and allotments.

Preface to 1990 (5th) Edition

The publication of the *Horticultural Show Handbook* in 1953 proved to be an important landmark in attempts to rationalise and stabilise rules and regulations governing the exhibition of flowers, fruits and vegetables at horticultural shows throughout Britain.

The guidance offered in the 1953 edition, subsequently updated in 1966, 1972 and 1981, has been very widely accepted by organisers of horticultural shows, exhibitors and judges and it has become the standard reference for all those who organise or take part in horticultural events.

The 1990 edition has been extensively revised after very wide consultation with Specialist Societies, Judges Guilds and many individual exhibitors. The Society is most grateful to all those who have contributed to the revision and to the members of the Committee responsible for the work, who dissected, re-assembled and checked the text to ensure its accuracy. In particular members of the National Vegetable Society were most helpful in giving generously of their expertise in the revision of the large section on vegetables and the Specialist Societies, too numerous to list individually, provided detailed comments on sections applicable to their own discipline.

Major changes both in format and content have been made. A new section on judging window boxes and hanging baskets has been added and the chapter on judging gardens and allotments has been simplified. Several groups of ornamental plants have been merged, for judging purposes, into one category to simplify this section and the chapter dealing with definitions has been made into a glossary and placed for reference at the end of the Handbook. In addition advice to organisers of shows has been updated and a note on the importance of taking out Public Liability insurance for shows added. For the first time colour illustrations have been used on the front and back covers and the text has been enlivened by the inclusion of a number of cartoons drawn by David Thelwell.

Whilst showing is often a serious business, calling for great expertise and skill on the part of those exhibiting and judging, it should also be an enjoyable experience for all who take part in the numerous shows, from village shows to Chelsea, that have made British Horticulture so much admired throughout the world.

We hope very much that this new edition of the Society's *Horticultural Show Handbook* will encourage and assist novice exhibitors and help to inspire seasoned veterans to achieve even greater heights of perfection in the future.

September 1990   *C D Brickell, Director General*

Horticultural Show Handbook Committee

CHAIRMAN	C D Brickell	Director General RHS
SECRETARY	A J Sawyer	RHS Staff
MEMBERS	H Baker	Fruit Officer, Wisley
	H J Dodson	RHS Fruit & Vegetable Committee Head Gardener, Chilton
	B Doe	RHS Staff
	R Fletcher	National Vegetable Society
	J Hillier	Nurseryman RHS Floral Committee
	G D Lockie	Past Chairman of RHS Fruit & Vegetable Committee
	S L Lord	RHS Fruit & Vegetable Committee Former Head Gardener, Shenley Hospital
	G W Nicholson	National Chrysanthemum Society Judge Middx Guild of Judges
	W M Robinson	Director of Robinsons Former President National Vegetable Society
	C Spires	Middx Guild of Judges
	R Waite	Glasshouse Superintendent, Wisley
	R Williams	Horticultural journalist Council Member National Vegetable Society

Any suggestions for amendments to the Handbook are welcomed and should be sent to The Secretary, Horticultural Show Handbook Committee, Vincent Square, London SW1P 2PE.

RULES

Unless otherwise stated in the schedule, the following rules apply to all competitions held by The Royal Horticultural Society.

These rules are suitable for incorporation in the schedules of many local horticultural societies if 'Committee' is substituted for 'Council'.

1. Eligibility of exhibitors On all questions regarding the eligibility of an exhibitor the decision of the Council shall be final.

2. Exhibits must be the property of the exhibitor Unless otherwise stated, all exhibits must be the property of the exhibitor and must have been in his possession for at least two months, unless some shorter period is specified in the schedule.

Note: It follows from this Rule that all exhibits should be entered in the name of the owner of the garden from which the exhibit came and he/she should sign the entry form in the place provided for the exhibitor's signature. Exhibits staged by a professional gardener but belonging to his/her employer should be entered in the employer's name.

3. Right to inspect gardens of competitors In order to be satisfied that the conditions governing competitive exhibits are fulfilled, the Council reserves the right to visit by commission, before or after a show, gardens from which plants, flowers, fruit or vegetables have been entered for competition.

4. Number of entries per household Unless otherwise stated in the schedule, two or more persons may not compete separately in the same class with produce from the same garden and/or allotment. This ruling does not apply to classes such as floral arrangement where exhibitors are allowed to use plant material which has not been grown by themselves. If members of a family wish to share the credit and prizes then the exhibits should be entered in joint names.

5. Acceptance of entries The Council reserves the right to refuse any entry and, in the event of such refusal, it is not required to give any reason or explanation.

6. Constitution of an exhibit Where a number or quantity of plants, flowers, fruit or vegetables is specified in the schedule for a class, vase, dish or collection, neither more nor less than the number or quantity may be shown and an exhibit will be disqualified by any excess or deficiency.

If before an exhibit is judged any excess or deficiency is noticed and considered to be the result of an accident and not of an attempt to deceive, the referee, steward or secretary may either give the exhibitor (if at hand) an opportunity to correct the mistake or correct it himself/herself but the officials shall not be under any obligation to do so and any disqualification resulting from an excess or deficiency shall be the exhibitor's responsibility. The judges may not correct any error but they may direct the attention of the referee, steward or secretary to it.

7. Constitution of dishes. Every dish must consist of one cultivar (variety) only, unless mixed dishes are permitted by the schedule. (*See page 23, paragraph 6.*)
Unless otherwise specified, a dish of the undermentioned fruits must consist of:

Apples	6	
Apricots	6	
Blackberries	25	
Blueberries (*bunches*)		
dish of not less than 15 oz (425g)		
and not more than 17 oz (480g)		
Bullaces	20	
Cherries	25	
Citrus Fruits, other than Kumquats	2	
Citrus Fruits, Kumquats	9	
Currants, Black, Red or White (*strigs*)		
dish of not less than 15 oz (425g)		
and not more than 17 oz (480g)		
Damsons	20	
Figs	3	
Gooseberries	25	
Grapes, indoor (*bunches*)	1	
Grapes, outdoor (*bunches*)	2	
Hybrid Cane Fruits e.g. Loganberries,		

Tayberries, and including Japanese Wineberries 25
Kiwi Fruits (Chinese Gooseberries) 6
Medlars 10
Melons 1
Nectarines 5
Nuts
 dish of not less than 15 oz (425g) and not more than 17 oz (480g)
Peaches 5
Pears 6
Pineapples 1
Plums 9
Quinces 6
Raspberries 25
Strawberries 20
Worcesterberries and Blackcurrant x Gooseberry hybrids e.g. Jostaberry (*on strigs*)
dish of not less than 15 oz (425g) and not more than 17 oz (480g)

Unless otherwise specified in the schedule, a dish of the undermentioned vegetables must consist of:

	In Collections	For Single Dishes
Artichokes, Chinese	8	8
Artichokes, Globe	3	3
Artichokes, Jerusalem	8	8
Asparagus	12	12
Aubergines	3	3
Beans, Broad	12	12

	In Collections	*For Single Dishes*
Beans, Dwarf French/Stringless	12	12
Beans, Runner	12	12
Beans, Climbing, other than Runner	18	18
Beetroot	6	6
Broccoli, Sprouting	18 *shoots*	18 *shoots*
Broccoli, Coloured-headed	3	3
Brussels Sprouts	20	20
Cabbages, Chinese	3	3
Cabbages, Green	3	3
Cabbages, Red	3	3
Cabbages, Savoy	3	3
Carrots	6	6
Cauliflowers, including White-heading 'Broccoli'	6	3
Celeriac	6	6
Celery	6	3
Chicory, Heads (Chicons)	9	9
Chili Peppers	18	18
Chives	1 *bunch**	1 *bunch**
Corn Salad (Lambs' Lettuce)	1 *bunch of 12 plants*	1 *bunch of 12 plants*
Courgettes	9	6
Cress	**	**
Cress, American or Land	1 *bunch of 12 plants*	1 *bunch of 12 plants*
Cucumbers	2	2
Dandelion, Blanched	6 *heads*	6 *heads*
Endive	3	3
Fennel, Florence	3	3
Garlic	12 *bulbs*	12 *bulbs*
Herbs	1 *bunch**	1 *bunch**
Kales	3	3
Kohl Rabi	6	6
Leeks	6	3
Leeks (pot)	4	2
Lettuces	3	3

---

*   *Chives or any herb should be represented by a neat bunch, sufficient to fill a 6-in vase (15 cm).*

**   *When shown in a collection of vegetables or saladings, mustard and cress should be exhibited in growth, not cut and be represented by not less than two 6-in pans (15cm) or their equivalent. If both mustard and cress are shown they will count as one item. Either may be shown alone if the exhibitor thinks fit. Rape will count as mustard.*

	In Collections	For Single Dishes
Marrows, including edible Squashes	2	2
Mushrooms	12	12
Mustard or Rape	** page 9	** page 9
Okra	6	6
Onions	9	5
Onions, Pickling	1 lb	1 lb
Onions, Green Salad	24	24
Parsnips	6	3
Peas	18 *pods*	12 *pods*
Peppers, Sweet	6	6
Potatoes	12	6
Pumpkins	1	1
Radishes	24	24
Rhubarb, Forced	6 *sticks*	3 *sticks*
Rhubarb, Natural	6 *sticks*	3 *sticks*
Salsify	6	6
Scorzonera	6	6
Seakale	8	8
Seakale Beet	*At least 15 and not more than 25 leaves*	*At least 15 and not more than 25 leaves*
Shallots	15	15
Spinach	*At least 15 and not more than 25 leaves*	*At least 15 and not more than 25 leaves*
Spinach, New Zealand	*At least 15 and not more than 36 tips*	*At least 15 and not more than 36 tips*
Spinach Beet	*At least 15 and not more than 25 leaves*	*At least 15 and not more than 25 leaves*
Swedes	6	3
Sweet Corn	6	3
Tomatoes	12	12
Turnips	6	3
Watercress	3 *bunches*	1 *bunch*

Unless otherwise specified it is suggested that the numbers given are used for RHS and the leading provincial shows.

8. The ripeness of fruit Apples, pears and gooseberries may be shown either ripe or unripe and all other fruits must be ripe, unless otherwise specified in the schedule. Over-ripeness will be regarded as a defect in any fruit.

9. Glasshouse grapes must be shown on stands unless some other method of staging is specified or permitted by the schedule.

10. The classification of dessert and cooking cultivars (varieties) of fruits Apples, pears and plums must be shown as dessert or cooking cultivars in accordance with the classified lists in the Appendix (page 140) unless the schedule provides otherwise. A new cultivar not listed in the Appendix may be shown and if necessary a classification as to whether it is dessert or culinary may be obtained from the Society beforehand.

11. Fruits classified as vegetables The following, though botanically classified as fruits, are for purposes of horticultural shows classified as vegetables:

Aubergines	Mushrooms
Beans	Okra
Capsicums (Sweet Peppers)	Peas
Chili Peppers	Pumpkins
Courgettes	Sweet Corn
Cucumbers	Tomatoes
Marrows	

12. The size of pots The diameter of a pot or pan is the inside measurement, made as close to the top as possible.

13. Stems to reach below the water In all classes where cut material is shown, all stems must reach below the water in the vase or other receptacle.

14. The naming of exhibits All exhibits should be correctly named. Errors in naming will not disqualify the entry but the judges should regard correctness and clearness of naming as telling in favour of an exhibit in a close competition.

If the exhibitor does not know the name of any cultivar the label should bear the words NAME UN-KNOWN.

All exhibits must be correctly labelled

When an unnamed seedling is shown (e.g. a seedling daffodil) the label should bear the word SEEDLING, and may be followed by an indicative number.

15. Exhibits not according to schedule Any exhibit which does not conform to the wording of the schedule (unless corrected in accordance with Rule 6) shall be disqualified and a steward or judge should write on the entry card 'Not according to schedule' (NAS) and add a factual note as to why it is marked NAS.

16. Only one prize in a class No exhibitor may be awarded more than one prize in any one class unless that is specifically permitted by the schedule. *(See also page 20, paragraph 18.)*

17. Prizes may be withheld Any prize may be withheld or modified if the exhibits are considered unworthy of the prize offered.

18. Decisions The decision of the judges shall be final on the relative merits of the exhibits but the Council reserves to the referees and to itself the decision on any other points in dispute.

19. Protests Any protest must be made in writing and delivered to The Secretary within one hour of the opening of the show to the public or by the time stated in the schedule, whichever is the earlier.

20. Alteration of exhibits After judging has taken place no exhibit or part of an exhibit may be altered or removed until the end of the show, except by special permission of The Secretary.

21. Liability for loss All exhibits, personal property, etc., shall be at the risk of the exhibitors and the Society shall not be liable for compensation for loss or damage from any cause whatsoever. Should a show for any cause not be held, no exhibitor shall have any claim on the Society.

Exhibitors will be wholly responsible for all claims made by their own employees under the Common Law or under any statute for compensation arising out of or in the course of such employment for injury or otherwise. The Society has no responsibility to any but its own employees.

22. Liability for injury to members of the public, guests, exhibitors and voluntary staff

Organisers of flower shows and similar events **are** liable for injury suffered by anyone in the course of a visit to or participation in the show and if the Society does not have public liability insurance cover then the liability lies with the officers of that Society who may be proceeded against. It is therefore essential that cover is provided either by the owners of the hall or building in which the show is held or by taking out a special policy on behalf of the Society.

SUGGESTIONS ON ORGANISATION

1. Exhibits from professional gardeners Anyone who is employed as a gardener, either full- or part-time, should be allowed to exhibit *in his/her own name* only produce from his/her own private garden or allotment and only in classes which are open to professional gardeners or to those who employ paid assistance in their gardens, as recommended in the next paragraph. (Produce from an employer's garden should be exhibited in the employer's name.)

2. The classification of exhibitors Local horticultural societies often wish to divide their schedules to make provision for two or more groups of exhibitors. Thus:

Group I   Amateurs who employ no paid assistance.
Group II   Amateurs who employ only one gardener and for not more than ten hours a week.
Group III   Amateurs who employ a part-time gardener for more than ten hours a week or who employ one full-time gardener or more than one full-time gardener.
Group IV   Professional gardeners.
Group V   Nurserymen, seedsmen and market-growers.

A person who belongs to Group I should also be allowed to compete against those in Groups II, III and IV and in any 'open' class or section.

A person who belongs to Group II should also be allowed to compete against those in Groups III and IV and in any 'open' class or section.

A person who belongs to Group III should also be allowed to compete against those in Group IV and in any 'open' class section.

Unless it is possible to provide a special section for Group IV, which is seldom the case, a professional gardener should be allowed to compete against the amateurs in Group III and in any 'open' class or section but *he/she should not be allowed to compete in a section provided expressly for Group I or Group II or in a section provided expressly for Groups I and II.*

For the horticultural traders in Group V a non-competitive section is usually best.

3. Payment of prize-money In order to encourage exhibits from those gardens where a gardener is employed, it is sometimes desirable to have a rule in the schedule to the effect that prize-money won by an amateur who employs a full-time gardener will be paid to the gardener (when known), unless the exhibitor has informed the

Secretary that he/she prefers some other arrangement. The exhibits should, however, invariably be entered in the name of the owner of the garden from which they come.

4. Right to inspect gardens of competitors   If, as is recommended, a society has a rule similar to Rule 3 reserving the right to inspect the gardens of competitors and it is decided to exercise that right, it does not follow that the gardens of all competitors need be visited. That would often be impracticable. One (or two) classes might be selected and the commission sent to the gardens of all who have entered in that class (or those classes). While at a garden, however, the commissioners should ask to be shown everything which the competitor proposes to exhibit and not merely the produce for the particular class.

Two experienced gardeners who are not exhibiting in the class or classes concerned form a suitable commission and they should be asked to submit a brief written report to the Secretary.

5. Entry-cards   Every exhibit should have an entry-card provided by the Secretary. A card 6 x $4^3/_4$ in (15 x 12 cm) is convenient. The face of the card should bear the name of the Society and/or Show and should have places for the number and description of the class, the name and address of the exhibitor, the name of the gardener (if any) and also a place where a label may be affixed if the exhibit should win a prize or be commended.

The back of the card should have places for the class number and the exhibitor's number and also a place for the judges to write 'First', 'Second', 'Third', 'Fourth', 'H.C.' (Highly Commended), or 'C' (Commended), if the exhibit merits one of those distinctions.

All the above-mentioned particulars, except the judges' assessment, should be on the card when it is handed to the exhibitor on his arrival to stage his exhibits. Each exhibitor should be responsible for the placing of the correct card with each of his/her exhibits, face downwards, and a steward should see that this is done.

A steward should follow the judges and as soon as possible after they have finished judging a class he/she should turn all the cards face upwards and at the same time affix appropriate labels to the faces of the cards of prize-winning and commended exhibits.

6. Labelling exhibits   The educational value of a show is greatly increased if all exhibits are labelled. For clearness, labels are best written or typed in capital letters. The general appearance of a show is improved if all labels are alike and it is recommended that competitors are provided with labels by the Secretary on receipt of entries. White cards about 3 x 1 in (7.5 x 2.5 cm) are suitable.

The judges should be asked to correct, whenever possible, labels which bear wrong names and to add, when possible, the name to a label which bears the words 'NAME UNKNOWN'.

7. Judges The qualifications of a good judge are integrity, familiarity with the kinds and cultivars of the items upon which he/she is to adjudicate and a knowledge of the skill required to grow and stage them. Just as High Court judges are drawn from those who have demonstrated their knowledge of the law as barristers, in a similar way good judges for a horticultural show are most frequently to be found among those people who are or have been successful exhibitors.

In order to avoid unconscious bias, the judges for a local show should, whenever possible, be drawn from outside the area which the show serves.

The number of judges should be determined by the number of exhibits and the time available for judging. If one group of judges is sufficient, the ideal number for a group is three. If one group is not enough the ideal is to have two or more groups of three. Where there are several groups of judges and each group consists of two, or some other even number, it is advisable to appoint a referee to give a casting vote if required.

One judge in each group should be nominated as responsible for the written record of the decisions of the group.

8. Referee or Referees Some shows, particularly those with strong competitions, require final decisions where judgements are in doubt. A referee or referees may be appointed of senior persons with all the qualifications of experienced judges.

In the absence of a referee, societies should nominate an experienced person who is not involved to arbitrate or confirm unresolved judgements.

9. Clearing show for judging Before the judging starts the hall or tent in which the exhibition is being held should be cleared of everyone except persons duly authorised by the committee to be present. Unless it is unavoidable, no official or any other person should be authorised

Before judging starts the exhibition area must be cleared of all unauthorised persons

to remain if he/she is a competitor. When a competitor is authorised to be present during judging, he/she must be careful to avoid being near any class in which he/she is interested while that class is being judged.

10. Stewards As the time available for judging is usually only sufficient for the judges to decide on the relative merits of the exhibits, one or more stewards should be appointed to ensure, as far as possible, that all exhibits are according to the schedule and that the judges have nothing to do beyond their proper duties.

If the number of entries in a particular class causes congestion in the space allotted on the show bench to the detriment of the exhibits, the steward should endeavour to ease the situation by adjusting the spacing in the adjoining class if there is room to do so. Any change a steward makes should be done with extreme care so as not to alter in any way the exhibitor's own staging.

Stewarding is an important function at any show. The steward is the link with the judge, the exhibitors and the show secretary. A steward's duties provide a very good training ground for those who wish to become either exhibitors or judges.

There are several important requirements for which stewards are responsible:

- Stewards should have checked weights/sizes, container dimensions or space and advised judges where entries were not in accordance with the schedule.

- Stewards should not have an interest in the particular section being judged or comment on the work of judging. At all times stewards should keep at a discreet distance from the judge. Stewards should make no comment except to answer any administrative queries raised by the judge, nor should they take part in any technical aspects of judging.

- Stewards should familiarise themselves with the schedule and layout of the classes in order to give clear and precise guidance to exhibitors on arrival, and be available to move exhibits where necessary.

- A steward should endeavour to see that all exhibits are staged in their appointed places and that each has its entry-card placed face downwards. He/she should also look out for mistakes which exhibitors are apt to make, especially when pressed for time, such as staging too few or too many specimens and, if possible, get the exhibitors to put matters right before the time fixed for the completion of staging. Before the judging begins the stewards should see that everyone leaves the exhibition hall or tent except those persons who are duly authorized by the committee to be present during the judging.

- Immediately before judging starts the show secretary should draw together judges and stewards and explain layout, duties and sections to all concerned.

- Stewards should ensure that the judge has knowledge of special prizes, awards and trophies that are to be given.

- Stewards should ensure that the judge does not inadvertently miss a class or part of a class.

- When the judge indicates that a class has been judged, the steward or a recorder is responsible for seeing that prize stickers have been fixed to the class cards; that comments why a class/exhibit has been marked 'NAS' have been made on the appropriate cards; and where points cards were used, that they have been completed by the judge. Prize cards should only be up-turned after the judge/judges have decided the Best Exhibit/Exhibits in the section/show or any special prizes. Finally, class cards must not be up-turned to display the appropriate prize sticker until all judging, including Best Exhibits, has been completed.

- When the show is open to the public, the presence of stewards is invaluable to patrol sections and stop theft and the handling of exhibits. An experienced steward is a great asset to a show and in terms of time and speed is also an asset to a judge.

11. Recording entries and prizewinners The following is a convenient system for keeping the records of a competitive show.

- A quarto- or foolscap-size book of horizontally lined paper is used and sufficient pages just inside the front cover are reserved for a list of the exhibitors, with addresses, allowing one (or two) lines for each exhibitor.

- Following the space allowed for the list of exhibitors, one page (or a half-page or two pages, according to the probable number of exhibitors) is reserved for each class in the schedule and a cutting from the schedule giving particulars of the class is pasted at the top of the page or half-page as the case may be.

- When an entry-form is received the exhibitor is given a number, which is written in some definite place on the form, say in the top right-hand corner. An entry is then made in the book in the place reserved for the list of exhibitors, with the exhibitor's number first and followed by his/her name and address.

- Then, turning to each of the pages reserved for the classes in which the exhibitor has entered, the number is written on the left-hand side of a line leaving the space on the right of this for a note of the prize if the exhibit should win one. The entry-form is then filed in alphabetical order of the exhibitor's surname.

- Therefore, with a minimum of writing, by referring to the file of entry-forms the Secretary can instantly find the number of any exhibitor whose name is known and by reference to the list of exhibitors in the book, the name of any exhibitor whose number is known.

- Each group of judges has a judges' card, on which the leading judge of the group makes a record of the group's decisions. The card has horizontal lines and seven vertical columns which, from left to right, are headed 'Class', 'First Prize', 'Second Prize', 'Third Prize', 'Fourth Prize', 'H.C.' and 'C'. Before the card is handed to the leading judge the first column is completed by the Secretary, allowing one horizontal line for each class. As soon as the judging of any class has been completed, the leading judge fills in the exhibitors' numbers in the columns provided for the prizewinners and also in the columns headed 'H.C.' and 'C' if any exhibit has been Highly Commended or Commended.

- When a group of judges has finished its work, the judges sign the card and the leading judge returns it to the Secretary. The notes of the exhibits which have won prizes or been commended are entered in the book and as soon as possible the correctness of the entries in the book is checked with the notes made by the judges on the backs of the cards of prizewinning and commended exhibits.

12. Exhibits adjudged equal If exhibits are examined carefully it should seldom be necessary to bracket any two as equally meritorious but when two exhibits are adjudged 'Equal First' the total amount of the first and second prizes should be divided equally between the two competitors and the next in order of merit should be awarded the third prize. The same principle applies to 'Equal Second', in which case there will be no third prize. If, when only three prizes are offered, two exhibits are 'Equal Third', either the third prize must be duplicated or the third prize must be divided between the two competitors.

13. The withholding of prizes Although in order to maintain a sufficiently high standard it is recommended that Rule 17 regarding the withholding of prizes be adopted, the power to withhold a prize should be exercised sparingly, as the whole object in offering prizes is to encourage exhibitors. If none of the exhibits in a class is worthy of the first prize, it is sometimes advisable to award the second prize for the best exhibit and the third prize for that which is next in order of merit. The judges may be empowered to decide whether an exhibit in a class is worthy of the prize but where a trophy is offered for the best exhibit in a section or in the whole show it may be advisable to ask the judges to make a recommendation and for the committee to reserve the decision to itself.

It is not desirable that a prize should be withheld solely on the ground that the exhibits are few in number. If an exhibit is worthy of the prize, the prize should be awarded, for it is not the exhibitor's fault that others have failed to exhibit.

14. Protests The time by which protests (which should be required to be in writing) must be received by the Secretary should be stated in the schedule and should be such that it is possible to consult the judges about any protests which concern their decisions or necessitate their reviewing any of the classes. The committee should, however, be willing to consider at any time a protest which alleges fraud.

In some circumstances it may be desirable to state in the schedule that any protest must be accompanied by a cash deposit which will be returned if the protest is considered by the committee to be justified.

15. Disputes When the committee of a local horticultural society is unable to decide a problem connected with a show, the matter in dispute may be submitted to The Royal Horticultural Society. The inquiry should be sent by the Secretary and not by any individual member of the local society. The letter, which must enclose a schedule of the show and give all the relevant facts, should be addressed to The Secretary, The Royal Horticultural Society, Vincent Square, London, SW1P 2PE.

In case of disputes the matter may be submitted to the RHS

16. Hardy plants Classes are often provided for 'hardy' plants. A hardy plant is one which is able to survive the average winter when grown in the open without protection but plants which can be grown in the open in some parts of the British Isles need shelter under glass in less favoured districts. If any question arises on this point in a competition, the exhibitor should be required to sign a statement that the plant in question has been grown in the open, without protective covering, for at least the twelve months before the show.

17. Best Bloom A special award for the Best Bloom shown in the horticultural classes may be required. For the purposes of such a competition, the strict definition of a bloom as a single open bloom or a flower head should be disregarded, so as to render eligible single spikes or inflorescences of such plants as delphiniums, gladioli and pelargoniums.

Best in Show At many shows there is a trophy for the Best in Show exhibit. This is often a problem to decide, especially where there are several judges involved in different sections of the show. It is better that awards are given for Best in Vegetable, Best in Flower and Best in Fruit sections. Where a society wishes to provide a Best in Show award, then section/specialist judges should each point their own Best in Section on a highest percentage basis prior to the judges assembling together to award Best in Show. Similarly, in awarding a Best in Section award, judges should point possible winners. A disqualified exhibit cannot be eligible for consideration for Best in Show but may be eligible for the award of a special prize at the discretion of the show committee. Individual dishes in collection classes are not eligible for Best in Show awards as they cannot be considered as exhibits in themselves, only as part of an exhibit.

18. Number of entries in a class Show organisers must ensure that judges and competitors are not in any doubt about the number of entries which any one individual may enter in any one class. The proper rule should be that if a competitor is only eligible to win one prize in one class then he may stage only one entry. It is the duty of all judges to award the prizes to the most meritorious exhibits in a class and their task should not be complicated by instructions to ignore certain entries because they have all been exhibited by the same exhibitor. The public, too, will not readily understand why 2nd and 3rd prizes in such classes have gone to exhibits which are clearly inferior to others that have received no prizes at all.

19. Multiple entry classes Societies may retain the option of allowing multiple entry classes and making all entries eligible for all prizes but this is only advisable when the organisers can be sure of strong support from a large number of competitors, a high standard of entries, and a long prize list. There is no reason why a show schedule should not contain one or more multiple entry classes while retaining the rule of one entry per exhibitor in the rest of the schedule.

20. The division of duties between Show Secretary, Steward and Judge

Show Secretary	Steward	Judge
Mark out the show benches.	See that exhibitors put the right exhibit in the right class and ensure that it is staged according to schedule.	Assess all exhibits as shown and award prizes as stated in the schedule including any special awards.
Ensure that the hall is open and ready for staging at the right time and remains open until the stated completion time.	Assist new exhibitors who are uncertain of classification or procedure.	Refer to steward and/or show secretary any exhibits which are wrongly staged, incorrectly labelled or not according to schedule.
Provide entry-cards and, where necessary, a supply of vases, plates, bowls, etc.	Interpret the wording of the schedule if required and inform the judges of the ruling before they begin judging.	Advise the show secretary after the show of ways in which the schedule might/should be improved.
Ensure that prize-monies are paid promptly after the show and that any trophies and special prizes reach their respective winners as quickly as possible.	Ensure that each exhibit staged has its proper entry-card correctly displayed.	
	Check immediately prior to judging that EVERY exhibit has been staged according to the schedule and remove any coverings or dust sheets.	
	Advise judges of any special awards or prizes. Check that every exhibit in each class has been judged.	
	Draw to the judges' attention any exhibit which is not according to schedule.	

SUGGESTIONS TO SCHEDULE-MAKERS

1. The use of terms Anyone concerned with the drafting of a schedule should become familiar with the definition of terms in common use and especially with the meaning of 'kinds' and 'cultivars' (varieties). (See pages 133 and 131.)

2. The time-table The following dates and times should be clearly stated in the schedule:

- The latest time for the receipt of entries.
- The time when staging must be started and the time by which it must be completed.
- The time judging will commence.
- The time when the show will be open for the admission of exhibitors and the public after the judging has been finished.
- The time when the show closes and when exhibitors may start to remove their exhibits.
- The time by which all exhibits and property of exhibitors must be removed.
- The date by which prize-money will be paid.

These times should be carefully decided, so that they may be strictly enforced without hardship to anyone.

3. The enforcement of rules, etc. It is not advisable to print such warnings as 'This rule will be strictly enforced', as such expressions imply that other rules will not be enforced.

4. The time for the receipt of entries In order to obtain the maximum number of entries it is advisable to make the last day for the receipt of entries as late as possible but sufficient time must be allowed between the receipt of entries and the staging of exhibits to allow the necessary clerical work to be done and the spaces for the various classes to be worked out. The interval between the last day for the receipt of entries and the opening day of the show should not, as a rule, be more than a week. It is sometimes advisable for the regulation on the matter to say: 'All entries should reach the Secretary not later than (date) but the Secretary may, at his/her discretion, accept a late entry up to, but not after, the day before the show.'

5. Rules The rules under which the show is to be conducted should be clearly stated in the schedule. If, in order to avoid expense, it is decided that all the rules set forth on pages 7-12 of this Handbook will not be printed in the schedule, there should be a statement in the schedule more or less as follows: 'The show will be conducted in accordance with the rules and standards contained in The Royal Horticultural Society's *Horticultural Show Handbook 1990*, except where, under this schedule, they obviously do not apply.'

There are, however, certain rules that should always appear in the schedule, i.e. those that appear on pages 7-12 under the following headings (with 'Committee' substituted for 'Council' when a committee is the governing body):

i   Exhibits must be the property of the exhibitor (page 7, rule 2.)
ii   Right to inspect gardens of competitors (page 7, rule 3.)
iii Only one exhibitor from one garden (page 7, rule 4.)
iv   Acceptance of entries (page 7, rule 5.)
v   Stems to reach below the water (page 11, rule 13.)
vi   The naming of exhibits (page 11, rule 14.)
vii Only one prize in a class (page 12, rule 16.)
viii Prizes may be withheld (page 12, rule 17.)
ix   Decisions (page 12, rule 18.)
x   Protests (page 12, rule 19.)
xi   Alteration of exhibits (page 12, rule 20.)
xii Liability for loss (page 12, rule 21.)

6. Constitution of dishes It is important that the schedule should make clear how many specimens constitute a dish of the various fruits and vegetables. The numbers or quantities ordinarily required at The Royal Horticultural Society's shows are detailed on pages 8 to 10, in Rule 7. These numbers and quantities are also suitable for the leading regional shows, for which the adoption of Rule 7 as it stands is recommended.

If it is wished to have a larger number or quantities than those specified in Rule 7, the schedule should (a) state the exact number or quantity required; or (b) say 'not more than ... fruits (or as the case may be) to a dish'; or (c) give the size of the receptacle, e.g. in classes for commercial growers the dimensions of an appropriate market-container.

At smaller shows the number or quantities specified in Rule 7 would often be too great. If, on the grounds of economy, it is not possible to print in the schedule tables similar to those in Rule 7, the number of specimens required should be stated in the wording of each class, thus:

Class 4   Black Currants, in bunches, 1 dish of between 7 and 9 oz (198 and 255g)
Class 6   Gooseberries, 1 dish of 20.
Class 21   Beetroot, Globe Type, 1 dish of 3.

Class 30   Lettuces, Cos, 1 dish of 2.

In the case of collections it may not be feasible to follow the same plan, but the difficulty can be overcome by a general rule as follows:

'Every dish must consist of one cultivar (variety) only, unless otherwise stated in the schedule. The numbers of specimens constituting dishes in a collection of fruit or vegetables must be those specified in the single-dish classes, unless otherwise specified in the schedule.'

7. The relative value of prizes   As far as possible the relative value of first, second and third prizes should be constant and in the ratio 4:3:2 or 3:2:1. The former is preferable because the first prize exhibit is not usually worth three times as much as the third and, if the 4:3:2 ratio is adopted, in the event of the award of a fourth prize being warranted, the amount of the prize can be automatically determined as the sum represented by one unit.

Thus if the 4:3:2 ratio is adopted and the first prize is, for example, £4, then the second should be £3, the third £2 and the fourth (if a fourth prize is awarded) £1.

The value of the prizes in a class should be related to what is involved in producing the required exhibit. Thus, if the first prize in a class calling for one dish of potatoes is £8, the first prize in a class calling for three dishes of potatoes should not be less than £20 and the first prize calling for six dishes should not be less than £40. Similarly, if the first prize for a dish of radishes or a dish of shallots is £6, then the first prize for a dish of peas or potatoes or onions should not be less than £8.

8. The point-value of prizes   When a cup or other trophy is offered for award to the most successful competitor in a show or in a section of a show, a competitor's degree of success is usually assessed by giving a point-value to the prizes.

The point-value principle has much to recommend it, provided that the point-value of a prize corresponds to the difficulty of winning the prize. But a flat rate, such as three points for any first prize, two points for any second prize and one point for any third prize, is not considered fair. The winner of the first prize in a comparatively difficult class (such as one for a collection of one dish of each of six kinds of vegetables) should get more points than the winner of the first prize in an easy class (such as one for a single dish of shallots). The number of points should be graduated in much the same way as money prizes are graduated and the point-value of the prizes in the various classes should be stated in the schedule.

9. The withholding of prizes   It is desirable that an appropriate standard for prizes should be established and should not be allowed to deteriorate. In order to do this it is recommended that Rule 17 (page 12) should be adopted and printed in the schedule, so that if the best exhibit in a class is not worthy of the first prize, the first prize need not be awarded. Similarly, the rule empowers the judges to withhold the second or, indeed, any prize.

On the other hand, it is not desirable that a schedule should stipulate that no prize or only certain prizes will be awarded in a class unless there are more than some specified number of entries. Whether a prize is awarded or not should depend solely on the merits of the exhibit.

10. More than one entry from a competitor in a class The practice of allowing competitors to stage more than one entry in a class yet only be eligible for one prize causes certain practical difficulties, both to the judges and organisers, and also confusion to the public visiting the show. Schedule-makers are strongly recommended not to adopt such a practice.

11. The numbering of classes To avoid the possibility of confusion the classes should be numbered in consecutive order (except as mentioned below) throughout a schedule; that is to say, no class number should appear twice, even if the schedule deals with two or more shows.

When a schedule contains two or more sections it may be helpful in avoiding unnecessary alterations and consequent expense in subsequent years if some numbers are omitted. Thus if Section I ends at Class 15, Section II might begin at Class 21 and so on. This would allow anything up to five classes to be added to Section I without necessitating the renumbering of the classes in Section II.

12. Salading and salad vegetables These are vegetables used as articles of food in either a raw or cooked state and served cold in salads. The kinds which may be used for horticultural show purposes are listed under 'Salading or salad vegetable' in the Glossary, page 137.

If it is desired that each exhibit in a class should consist of four kinds of such vegetables as beetroot, celeriac, cucumbers, kohl rabi, lettuces and tomatoes, then the schedule should call for 'Four kinds of salading or salad vegetables'.

13. The use of 'Genus', 'Species' and 'Hybrid' For the purposes of competitions at the majority of horticultural shows the words 'kind' and 'cultivar' are recommended as being not only adequate but also the most satisfactory terms to use in the classification of flowers and ornamental plants as well as fruit and vegetables. However, those terms are not always sufficiently precise for competitions in connection with alpines, cacti, orchids, succulents, shrubs or trees. For such competitions the terms 'genus', 'species' and 'hybrid' may also be used.

14. 'Distinct', 'Similar' and 'Dissimilar' The words 'distinct', 'similar' and 'dissimilar' are often used in schedules. Sometimes they are intended to bear their ordinary meaning and in others a quite different meaning. Even if they are intended to bear their ordinary meaning their use is undesirable because they lack precision, for what is 'distinct' to one person is not to another. Thus the apples 'Charles Ross' and 'Peasgood's Nonsuch' are quite distinct to many people, while to other people they are so similar that they cannot tell them apart until the differences are pointed out. On the other hand, when the words are used to convey a meaning other than that which they ordinarily bear, the intended meaning is misunderstood. Consequently, it is recommended that the words 'distinct', 'similar' and 'dissimilar' are not used in the specifications for classes in schedules.

15. 'Should' and 'Must' The word 'should' is often used where 'must' is intended and vice versa. 'Should' leaves what follows optional; 'must' makes what follows obligatory. The inadvertent substitution of the one word for the other may cause an exhibit to be disqualified or free it from liability to disqualification.

16. The ripeness of fruit Unless the schedule states that the fruit must be ripe, apples and pears may be shown either ripe or unripe; therefore, if only ripe apples and pears are required, the schedule must say so.

17. Annuals and biennials Many perennial plants are commonly cultivated as annuals; that is to say, they are raised from seed, flowered and discarded within twelve months. The difficulty of distinguishing between annuals, biennials and perennials is so great that it is recommended that instead of having a class or classes calling for 'annuals' and/or 'biennials', such classes should call for 'flowers raised from seed during the twelve months preceding the Show'. In such a class it would be permissible to exhibit not only true annuals and biennials but also perennials (such as antirrhinums and petunias) which are often cultivated as annuals.

18. Carrot and potato classes Exhibitors and judges are often in doubt about the cultivars which may be shown without fear of disqualification in classes for these vegetables. This uncertainty may in part be caused by different views about the classification of cultivars (either by shape or by colour) and also by the use of wording in classes which is open to an unduly limiting interpretation. Opinions may differ as to the identity of 'intermediate' carrots or 'kidney-shaped' potatoes; exhibitors may not know in which classes in a show they should be entered and judges may disqualify them for being in the wrong classes.

Schedule-makers are accordingly advised to adopt as simple wording as possible for carrot and potato classes and as a guide the wording for classes at The Royal Horticultural Society's competitions is given below. The Society provides two classes for each vegetable in addition to collection classes. 'Intermediate' carrots are classed as long, pointed types. No attempt is made to provide separate potato classes for each of the different shapes nor is a rigid colour classification given. If an exhibitor has specimens of a normally 'coloured' cultivar of potato which show no colour, he/she is able to show them in the 'white' class.

'Carrots, a long, pointed cultivar.'
'Carrots, other than a long, pointed cultivar.'
'Potatoes, white, of any shape.'
'Potatoes, coloured, of any shape.'

19. Onion classes Uncertainty often exists amongst judges and exhibitors when onion classes are judged. Schedule-makers are recommended not to use such wording as 'Onions, spring-sown cultivars', 'Onions, autumn-sown cultivars', or 'Onions, cultivars grown from onion sets'. Difficulties occur when separate classes of this kind are included, as judges are often unable to determine the origin or method of culture of bulbs entered for classes under these headings. In assessing onions equal points may be awarded for condition, size, form and uniformity, and undue emphasis should not be placed on any one of these features, particularly size. When wording onion classes it is advisable to consider examples similar to the following:

'Onions, 1 dish.'
'Onions, excluding Green Salad or Pickling Onions, 1 dish.'
'Onions, no bulb to exceed 8 oz (225g), 1 dish.'

Note: Onions for early shows should have foliage trimmed to not more than 3 in (7.5 cm) from the neck of the bulb.

Societies are advised to make available an accurate set of scales for the use of exhibitors, stewards and judges, both before and during judging.

20. Tomato classes It is often difficult for judges to distinguish between indoor- and outdoor- grown tomatoes where the latter have had some form of protection, such as plastic sheeting. It is therefore suggested that schedule-makers offer a class for 'Tomatoes, ordinary cultivars' and, where desired, another class for 'Tomatoes, small-fruited and novelty cultivars', to include for example, multi-coloured cultivars.

21. **'Own Foliage'** In a class for 'Sweet Peas, two cultivars, one vase of each, nine sprays to a vase, arranged with own foliage', the words 'own foliage' mean that the foliage must be that of the cultivar with which it is shown. What, however, the words were intended to mean was 'Sweet Pea foliage only'. A similar form of words should be used in any similar circumstances, e.g. in classes for carnations and daffodils.

22. **Stocks** It is recommended that classes for stocks should call for spikes and not for plants with roots.

23. **The use of the words 'and' and 'or'** Schedules sometimes contain some such class as 'Hardy and Half-hardy Flowers, 6 kinds, 1 vase of each'. If in such a class an exhibitor staged six kinds of hardy flowers it would not be according to the schedule; nor would an exhibit consisting of six kinds of half-hardy flowers. Yet in such a case it is not usually the schedule-maker's intention to exclude either but to allow both if the exhibitor so desires.

It will be seen, however, that had the schedule said 'Hardy or Half-hardy Flowers' the position would have been no better, for an exhibit which included both hardy and half-hardy flowers would not be according to schedule, though it was not the schedule-maker's intention to exclude such an exhibit.

If, as in this instance, the intention is to allow

(a) an exhibit consisting solely of hardy flowers; and

(b) an exhibit consisting solely of half-hardy flowers; and

(c) an exhibit consisting partly of hardy and partly of half-hardy flowers;

then the class should read:

'Hardy and/or Half-hardy Flowers, 6 kinds, 1 vase of each.'

24. **The wording of classes.** The following are examples of well-worded classes:

A COLLECTION OF 6 DISHES OF RIPE FRUIT, not fewer than 4 kinds, not more than 2 dishes of a kind, nor more than 1 dish of a cultivar.

PLUMS, 4 CULTIVARS, 2 dessert and 2 cooking, 1 dish of each.

A COLLECTION OF 6 KINDS OF VEGETABLES, 1 dish of each.

POTATOES, 3 CULTIVARS, 1 dish of each.

A COLLECTION OF 6 KINDS OF HARDY PERENNIAL FLOWERS, trees and shrubs excluded, one 9-in* (23 cm) vase of each.

A COLLECTION OF 6 KINDS OF HARDY PERENNIAL FLOWERS, trees,

---

* *If vases of a standard size cannot be provided, the maximum size of vase permitted should be stated in the rules in terms of the diameter of the mouth of the vase or the maximum size of the exhibits indicated in some other way.*

shrubs and plants having bulbs, corms or tubers excluded, one 9-in* (23 cm) vase of each.

Trees and/or Shrubs, in Bloom, 3 Kinds, roses excluded, one 9-in* (23 cm) vase of each.

Flowers Raised from Seed during the preceding 12 months, grown in the open, 6 kinds, one 9-in* (23 cm) vase of each, colour variation allowed.

25. Badly worded classes The following are examples of badly worded classes:

A Collection of 6 Kinds of Fruit

Comment: As the number of dishes is not stated, more than six dishes might be shown.

A Collection of 6 Dishes of Ripe Fruit

Comment: As neither the number of kinds nor the number of cultivars is stated it would be permissible to show six cultivars of apples or of any other kind or even six dishes of one cultivar of apple or pear or plum.

A Collection of 6 Cultivars of Ripe Fruit, 1 dish of each

Comment: As the number of kinds is not stated it would be permissible to show one dish of each of six cultivars of apple, pear or plum or one dish of each of six kinds, e.g. apples, pears, plums, damsons, peaches and nectarines.

Plums, 4 Cultivars

Comment: As nothing is said on the matter, all four might be dessert cultivars or cooking cultivars or there might be three dessert cultivars and one cooking cultivar; and as nothing is said about the number of dishes, any number of dishes in excess of four might be shown.

A Collection of 6 Dishes of Vegetables

Comment: As neither the number of kinds nor the number of cultivars is stated it would be permissible to show one dish of each of six cultivars of potatoes or any other one kind or even six dishes of one cultivar of potato or carrot or tomato.

Potatoes, 3 Dishes

Comment: As the number of cultivars is not stated it would be permissible to show three dishes of one cultivar or two dishes of one cultivar and one dish of another.

Perennials, 6 Vases.

Comment: As flowers are not mentioned the plants need not be in bloom and it would be permissible to include ferns. As the number of kinds is not stated an exhibit might include several vases of one

---

*   *If vases of a standard size cannot be provided, the maximum size of vase permitted should be stated in the rules in terms of the diameter of the mouth of the vase or the maximum size of the exhibits indicated in some other way.*

kind of plant. As there is nothing to indicate the contrary, it would be permissible to include trees and shrubs and, in fact, any plant, hardy or tender, except annuals and biennials.

A VASE OF MIXED CUT FLOWERS

Comment: As no indication is given, it would be permissible (i) to mix perennials, biennials and annuals, (ii) to include as few as two or as many as twenty different kinds and (iii) to include only different cultivars (varieties) of one kind, such as phlox. The judge's task in comparing exhibits from the wide range possible under such wording would be very difficult. Some guidance as to the number of different flowers required should be given and it should be made clear whether different cultivars of the same kind would be eligible or whether only one example of each kind may be included.

26. Any other Fruit/Vegetable Classes These classes are intended to allow exhibitors to show fruit or vegetables which they are not able to enter in any other class in the schedule. The items shown are normally those for which the schedule-makers feel there would be insufficient entries to justify the particular fruit or vegetable having a class of its own.

Within such a class there is the probability that a wide diversity of kinds will be entered each with a different point value according to the recommendations given on pages 50 to 84. Points are based to a large extent on the degree of difficulty involved in producing a high quality crop for the show bench and it is not desirable that fruits or vegetables which command high points should be judged against those which are easy to grow and therefore command low points. To avoid this situation schedule-makers are advised to include two 'any other' classes as follows:

Any other fruit/vegetable with a point value of up to 14 points.

Any other fruit/vegetable with a point value of 15 or more points.

It is appreciated that in small shows on a restricted budget there might only be sufficient prize-money for one 'any other' class and where this is the case the judge concerned should be asked to make due allowance for the degree of difficulty of cultivation in his/her assessment. The pointing system should only be used as a guide in such classes and other factors such as quality and presentation should be taken into consideration.

SUGGESTIONS TO EXHIBITORS

1. The schedule An exhibitor should read the schedule very carefully, including all the rules. If anything is not clear he/she should write to the Secretary immediately. The solution of problems should not be left until the show day, as exhibitors and officials are then particularly busy.

2. Dates and times The dates and times given in the schedule should be carefully noted, particularly:

(i) the latest day and time for the receipt of entries;
(ii) the time when staging may be started and the hour by which it must be finished; and
(iii) the time when the show closes and the hour by which exhibitors must have removed their property.

In his/her own interest every exhibitor should do his/her utmost to adhere to the time-table and also to avoid doing things at the last moment.

3. Entry-form An exhibitor should see that his/her intentions are stated quite clearly on the entry-form, that the name and address are legible and that the form reaches the Secretary by the appointed day but earlier if possible. If the entries arrive over a period of a week or so it is much easier to cope with the secretarial work than if nearly all the entries arrive on the last day.

4. Prizes not everything When selecting the classes in which to compete, an exhibitor should bear in mind that there is more honour in exhibiting well in a strongly contested class without winning a prize than in winning a prize in a class where there is little or no competition.

The educational value of an exhibit staged in a poorly contested class, provided that the exhibit is of good standard, should not, however, be overlooked.

5. Avoid making too many entries No competitor should put in an entry for a class unless he/she is reasonably sure that he/she will be able to stage an exhibit in it. Those who make numerous entries and fail to produce the exhibits or cancel the entries at the last moment make it difficult or impossible for the staging to be allocated as it should be, with the result that in some classes the exhibits are crowded and elsewhere there are vacant spaces.

6. Encourage beginners If, when looking through a schedule, it occurs to an exhibitor that a friend is a successful grower of some particular flower, fruit or vegetable for which there is a class, the friend should be persuaded to enter. If the friend has never exhibited before and needs advice, he/she should be helped as much as possible. Similarly, if when staging exhibits a beginner is encountered, the experienced exhibitor should give any assistance needed. If, when putting up exhibits, one exhibitor notices that a competitor has inadvertently made a mistake (such as staging the wrong number of specimens or omitting to put labels or entry-cards in position) attention should be drawn to the matter while there is time for it to be put right.

7. Allow ample time for staging Plenty of time should be allowed for putting up exhibits and for finishing the work well before the hour fixed in the schedule for the completion of staging. A last-minute rush should be avoided, for it is during such times of stress that an exhibitor inadvertently puts in one too many specimens or makes some other easily avoidable mistake which results in disqualification, disappointment and what may seem like the loss of a year.

8. Labels and entry-cards Labels with the names of the cultivars to be exhibited should be prepared at home in order to save time on the show day. It is best to use block letters. On arrival at the place of the exhibition an exhibitor should immediately procure entry-cards from the Secretary or whoever has been deputed to deal with them. Both labels and entry-cards should be placed in position on the exhibits in good time and care should be taken to see that they correspond to the exhibits.

9. 'Should' and 'Must' As many schedule-makers inadvertently put 'should' when they mean 'must' and many judges do not distinguish between the meanings of the two words, if the schedule says 'should' it is often wise for an exhibitor to act, if possible, as if the word were 'must'.

10. The number of specimens required Particular attention should be paid to the number of specimens for which the schedule asks, as an exhibit consisting of either more or less will be liable to disqualification on the ground that it is 'not according to schedule' (NAS).

11. Uniformity of specimens constituting an exhibit In any competitive exhibit, but especially in one of fruit or vegetables, uniformity of the specimens constituting it is important. Therefore it is unwise to weaken an exhibit by mixing large specimens with others which are smaller yet large enough to be meritorious.

12. Be absent during judging If they have not already done so, at the time fixed for the completion of staging all exhibitors should leave the exhibition hall or marquee without delay and not return until the time fixed for the re-admission of exhibitors.

13. Be a sportsman

The judges' decision, whatever it may be, should be accepted with good grace. An exhibitor who has failed to get a prize and cannot at once see why, should search calmly and patiently for the cause of his/her competitors' success in order to achieve better results another time.

The judges' decision, whatever it may be, should be accepted with good grace

14. Protests should

not be made lightly but only if, after careful consideration, an exhibitor feels sure that a mistake has been made. In those circumstances a courteously worded appeal should be made in writing to the Secretary, who will see that it receives proper attention. The final decision should be accepted without question.

If, however, the time fixed in the schedule for the receipt of protests has passed before the mistake or supposed mistake is discovered, the judges' decision should be accepted without comment and no action taken.

15. Liability for loss
The organisers usually very wisely stipulate in the schedule that exhibits and other property of exhibitors will at all times be at the risk of the exhibitors because, especially when exhibits are being removed at the close of a show, it is quite impossible for the organisers to ensure the safety of exhibitors' property. Therefore each exhibitor should arrange to take charge of his/her exhibits etc. immediately after the hour fixed for the closing of the show arrives and if he/she cannot do so personally, arrangements should be made beforehand for someone else to do so.

16. The preparation and presentation of produce at shows
All exhibits should be staged in accordance with the rules and schedule as attractively as possible. In close competition points for arrangement may be the deciding factor, and in any case a judge cannot fail to be favourably influenced by good presentation. Always take a few extra specimens to the show in case of accident, and before leaving

the show bench check that the correct numbers have been staged so that your exhibit is not marked NAS ('Not according to schedule').

17. The preparation and presentation of flowers
(See also page 33, paragraph 16.)

Preparation before cutting Starting two or three weeks before a show, keep the soil moist by giving generous quantities of water at each application, especially if the weather is hot and dry. In many cases the removal of unwanted weak sideshoots or buds will aid development of the central or main flowers. If possible, and permissible under the schedule, protect blooms such as asters, chrysanthemums, gladioli, lilies and pansies to prevent spotting caused by heavy rain, hail damage or splashing from the soil. If light conditions are not good, make sure pot plants have sufficient space in which to develop and turn the pots frequently to avoid lop-sided growth. Pot plants such as calceolarias and cinerarias should be lightly shaded otherwise there is a risk of the flowers fading in colour or scorching.

Cutting Before cutting and exhibiting, carefully study the show schedule and note the requirements for each class you intend to enter. Cut for a show in the evening or early morning when the flowers and foliage are cool and not affected by heat. Flower stems should be cut as long as possible. Make a slanting cut at the end of the stalk as this will assist the uptake of water. Certain flowers, e.g. some cultivars (varieties) of chrysanthemums and penstemons, are particularly reluctant to absorb water and in these cases slitting the cut stems 3 in (7.5 cm) upwards from the base or dipping the severed ends in boiling water will improve matters. Other plants, notably poppies, do not seal easily after cutting and should have their stalk ends seared in a naked flame to prevent wilting.

As cutting proceeds, carefully label each item, for mistakes easily occur which can affect your chances in competition and cause disappointment. Avoid handling show material any more than is necessary. Carry the cut stems with blooms facing downwards, keeping the plants away from draughts or bright sunshine as much as possible. Try to cut sufficient material to allow some latitude when final selection is made at the time the exhibit is staged.

When cutting is completed, remove undeveloped sideshoots, unopened buds and some of the lower leaves as these will often divert water from the stems and open flowers to be exhibited. The cut stems should be plunged upright up to their necks in deep containers of clean water. It is a considerable advantage to do this overnight, placing the containers in a cool position from which light is mostly excluded because stems are drawn towards the light and consequently they can become curved or bent. If this is not possible, wrap a sheet of newspaper round the material and tie at the top to exclude light. Take care to see the covering paper is tied well above the uppermost flowers and that it does not absorb any water from the container. Flowers treated in this way will be encouraged to expand before a show begins. Pot plants should receive enough water so they are fresh at the time of showing.

Where the show schedule permits, stems of plants in this section are neatly tied, using individual supports which should be made as inconspicuous as possible.

Transit to a show Place the material, either flat or upright, in containers of sufficient size to prevent the flowers becoming squashed or damaged during the journey. Pack cotton wool, soft paper or other similar material between specimens to prevent movement and buffeting in transport. Ensure that pot plants are securely supported to prevent excessive sway and subsequent breakage. Always allow enough time for the journey so that if delay should occur there will still be time to stage the exhibit without undue haste.

Staging exhibits at a show Remove any damaged flowers together with discoloured or broken leaves which may have occurred as a result of the journey. Cut a portion from the base of all flower stems to assist the uptake of water, making sure that the length of stalk retained is appropriate for the size of vase or container you propose to use. Check that all containers are filled with water otherwise plants in your exhibit may wilt during the show. Strive to produce exhibits of good balance with flowers of even size and quality which are accommodated in containers of suitable proportions. Label exhibits clearly, preferably using block capital letters for cultivar (variety) names but defer this operation until last if it is intended to apply a final spray of water over the exhibit just before judging starts.

18. The preparation and presentation of fruit
(*See also page 33, paragraph 16.*)

Preparation Initial preparation should begin well beforehand. Protect against frost and cold winds in the spring. Both may destroy, mar or blemish all kinds of fruit. Where a heavy set has been obtained, thinning must be considered. Apples, pears, plums, peaches, apricots, figs, grapes, gooseberries and strawberries all benefit from thinning. Thin in stages, especially those kinds of fruit which shed some of their fruitlets naturally, e.g. apples and pears, bearing in mind that early thinning has the most beneficial effect on size. Remove the small, blemished and mis-shapen fruits first. With many apple cultivars the 'king fruit' or centrally placed apple in the cluster is mis-shapen.

The fruits that require plenty of sunshine to bring out their characteristic colours should not be over-shaded. As they begin to ripen, they should be exposed gradually to more sunshine by the judicious removal of leaves and the tying back of overhanging foliage. Peaches and nectarines may be tilted towards the sun by means of small pieces of wood placed behind them. There is the risk of sun scald on glasshouse-grown fruits and grapes and figs in particular must have the protection of their foliage. The aim should be to obtain sufficient uniformly ripened specimens for the class or classes to be entered.

Protect against birds well before the fruits ripen. Some growers protect individual fruits in muslin or perforated, clear polythene bags and often the skin finish can be improved in this way. Some fruits are liable to split when almost ripe and others may be spoilt by heavy rains. Black polythene over the soil surface of the rooting area may sometimes mitigate splitting.

Picking Pick as near to show time as practicable. Black, white and red currants and Jostaberries should be picked with the strigs intact choosing the longest strigs with the largest fruits. Grapes should be picked as a complete bunch and each bunch should be cut with a piece of lateral shoot on either side of the stalk to form a 'T' handle. Melons should be cut in the same way. Apples, pears, plums and allied fruits, cherries, apricots, quinces, figs, medlars, blackberries and allied fruits, gooseberries, raspberries and allied fruits, loganberries and strawberries should be picked with the stalks intact. Filberts, cobnuts and walnuts must be shown without husks. Peaches and nectarines may be gathered by cutting a section of the bearing branch but should be shown without branch wood. Handle the fruits as little and as gently as possible and by their stalks so that the natural bloom where present, e.g. on grapes, plums and some apples, is not spoilt. Use scissors rather than fingers to remove soft fruits. In wet weather raspberries may be left on the canes and whole pieces of the fruit-bearing canes brought under cover and placed in water, until dry enough to pick. Strawberries may be kept dry by covering with cloches or by placing individual fruits on the plants in jars but care should be taken to avoid damage by excessive heat.

Selection The desirable qualities of each kind of fruit are set out in the chapter 'The Judging of Fruits', pages 49 to 61. Choose only fruits as near to perfection as can be found. The fruits should be fresh, uniform, free from blemish and characteristic in shape and colour. Refer to the show schedule to see what is required, but pick more than is necessary so that reserves are available when staging. Do not use over-ripe fruits. Under-ripe fruits should also be avoided, except where allowed in certain classes (see page 49, Condition).

Packing Pack carefully. Wood wool, cotton wool, tissue paper and newspapers are all suitable materials to use. Soft fruits may be damaged by their own weight; avoid packing too many in one container. Hard fruits are best wrapped individually in soft tissue. Keep in a cool place.

Presentation and staging Aim for a neat attractive presentation, symmetrical if possible. Do not polish the fruits. Where applicable, the stalks should always point away from the front of the table. In staging small fruits, the well of the plate is best filled with soft tissue paper and then the whole of the top covered, tucking the surplus paper under the plate. Use only white tissue paper, unless otherwise stated in the schedule.

Apples and similar-shaped fruits (including some pears) should be staged with the eye uppermost, stalk end downwards, placing one fruit in the centre and the remainder around it. The centre fruit can be raised by placing a cushion of white tissue beneath it.

Berries look most attractive if placed in lines so that they can be easily counted. The stalks and calyces should look green and fresh and all point one way. Reject malformed and damaged fruits.

Currants The strigs should be intact and laid roughly parallel, the bottom of the strigs to the front of the plate. Mound the fruit in the centre.

Grapes Unless some other method of staging is specified or permitted by the schedule, glasshouse grapes should be staged on stands and should be pulled well up on to the board. Outdoor grapes grown for winemaking may be shown on plates.

Most pears, pear-shaped quinces and figs are best arranged around the perimeter of the plate with the stalks towards the centre.

Plums, cherries and similar-shaped fruits are best laid out in lines across the plate. It is important that the bloom is not disturbed and the stalks are intact.

Finally, before leaving the table, clear up any surplus packing material, debris, etc. and check that the entry strictly conforms to the show schedule, is looking its best and is labelled.

19. The preparation and presentation of vegetables
(See also page 33, paragraph 16.)
All vegetables should be properly prepared for showing. Before handling it is suggested that the exhibitor's finger nails are trimmed to prevent damage to the produce. Root vegetables should be carefully washed to remove soil but in no circumstances should oil or similar substances be applied in an attempt to enhance their appearance. Wash with a soft cloth and plenty of water; brushing will damage the skin and spoil the appearance of the exhibit. On other

kinds retain the natural 'bloom' wherever possible. All vegetables should be given a thorough watering well before harvesting for the show and should be handled carefully during preparations.

Vegetables should be staged as attractively as possible on plates or direct on to the table in a 'wheel' formation, e.g. peas; in rows, e.g. runner beans; or in pyramidal form, e.g. carrots.

Beetroot, Carrots, Parsnips, Turnips and Swedes should have the tops cut off leaving approximately 3 in (7.5 cm) and leaf stalks should be neatly tied. With beetroot it is advisable to cut a couple of spare roots to check the colour, absence of white zones and, in turnips and swedes, to check freedom from internal breakdowns or discolourations.

Beans and Peas should be carefully cut off the vine with scissors leaving some stalk attached.

Cabbages and Cauliflowers should be shown with approximately 3 in (7.5 cm) of stalk remaining.

Parsnips and long-pointed Carrots The soil or growing media should be soaked prior to careful lifting to ensure complete retention of the root.

Asparagus Pea/Petit Pois/Mangetout Peas Select fresh pods of approximately 2–3 in (5–7.5 cm) in length and of good colour. The pods should snap in half easily.

Artichokes, Globe Disbud the lateral heads leaving only the large main head. Stage heads on a plate, stalks to the centre.

Aubergines Cut the fruit carefully and stage on a plate in a pyramid shape, being careful to retain the natural skin condition. The nose ends should point towards the edge of the table.

Beans, Broad Exhibit pods of even green colour, discarding old specimens which often contain beans with a blemished black eye. Stage all pods lengthwise across a plate, with stalks at one end, tails at the other.

Beans, Dwarf and Stringless Size of pod is less important than tenderness and quality. Discard tough fibrous specimens. Stage on a plate in a straight line for easy counting and uniformity; check the stalks are all at the top with tails to the front.

Beans, Runner Stage a uniform-sized exhibit. Avoid poorly coloured, coarse specimens and specimens with wasp waists and poor shape. Do not adversely affect your chance in competition by including old, fibrous and poddy specimens and the one or two extra long specimens. Cut from the vine with scissors. Exhibit pods neatly across a plate or directly on the bench; stalks all to one end, tails facing the other, and all one way. With all beans it is advisable to snap one or two spare pods to check condition and interior freshness.

Beetroot Select roots of even size; for round beetroot about the size of a tennis ball, for long beetroot as for parsnips. Avoid specimens with poor skin colour at the base of the root or which do not have a single small tap root. Small side roots should be removed. Take care in washing as all marks will show up clearly after a few hours.

Brussels Sprouts Cut off main stem with a knife, all stalks to be nearly the same length. Choose tightly closed sprouts of uniform size. Do not remove too many outer leaves otherwise depth of colour is reduced.

Cabbages Choose solid heads of equal size with good waxy bloom. Reject split specimens and those damaged by pests. Remove only minimum of outer discoloured leaves. Stage with approximately 3 in (7.5 cm) of stalk, heads towards the front.

Carrots Avoid pale-coloured specimens or those which have turned green at the top. Select uniform roots of good colour.

Cauliflowers Reject pest-damaged, discoloured, split, loose or uneven-sized heads. Stage with approximately 3 in (7.5 cm) of stalk or as indicated in the schedule. Just prior to staging, trim back leaves so that they match the level of the outside of the curd. Cover the exhibit with clean paper or cloth to exclude light, but remove immediately before the start of judging.

Celery Choose only heads that have no diseased or pest-damaged foliage and that have not been damaged by slugs. Reject specimens showing flower heads forming. Place a tie round the base of the leaves to prevent breaking and clean by a continuous flushing with water; ensure all worms are removed. Before staging, neatly trim off the roots, leaving a pointed butt end. In dish classes where few heads are required, lay them flat on the show bench. In collection classes the specimens are enhanced by display on a backboard. To exclude the light cover with clean paper or damp cloth which must be removed immediately prior to judging.

Courgettes Select young, tender, shapely and uniform fruits not less than 4 in (10 cm) or greater than 6 in (15 cm) long, in any colour. Stage flat.

Cucumbers Fruits should be completely matched and of a good, fresh green colour with flowers still attached and waxy bloom undisturbed. The flower end should be completely developed, the barrel well shaped and with a short handle. Display specimens flat on the show bench.

Garlic   Clean off all soil fragments, dry completely. Reduce the dried stem to about 1 in (2.5 cm). Stage bulbs as complete specimens; do not divide segments.

Florence Fennel   Roots should be neatly trimmed off and side foliage trimmed back to approximately 3 to 4 in (7.5 – 10 cm), but with terminal foliage retained. Stage on a plate as an overlapping triangle.

Kohl Rabi   Choose tender, fresh, small-leaved specimens about billiard ball size (approximately 2 in or 5 cm in diameter), but no larger than a tennis ball. Trim roots neatly. Cut side foliage back to not more than 2 in (5 cm) and retain the terminal foliage. Stage in clean condition, but do not wash, and retain the natural bloom.

Leeks   Specimens should be comparable in length, in good condition and solid (i.e. firm and compact throughout the length of the barrel) and a good, uniform blanch without bulbousness at the base. Excessive stripping of outer leaves should be avoided, otherwise unsightly ribbing is exposed. In dish classes preferably stage the leeks to lie flat on the bench with the roots to the front, neatly teased out and well cleaned. Ensure that stem (barrel), leaves (flags) and roots (beard) are flushed clean with tap water which should not be allowed to run between the leaves leaving unsightly soil particles. Avoid soft, discoloured specimens or evidence in the stem and leaves of rust disease. Place specimens in collections vertically on a backboard, complementing celery where shown in length. Bind in the leaves to an appropriate length. Check all specimens for evidence of formation of a flower head, rejecting such specimens.

Some schedules have classes for intermediate leeks, i.e. where the blanch is over 6 in (15 cm) and under 14 in (35 cm).

Pot leeks call for a 6-in (15 cm) maximum blanch from root base to 'tight button', i.e. the point where the lowest leaf breaks the circumference of the blanched stem. Size should be of a maximum cubic capacity.

Nomenclature used by the National Pot Leek Society:

Barrel - the shaft or stem of the plant.

Blanch - that part of the stem which is blanched.

Beard - the roots.

Button - the point on the barrel of the plant where the lowest leaf breaks the circumference.

Flags - the leaves.

Veil - a thin white skin that forms across the bottom of well-grown leeks and which, where present, is included in the measurements.

Lettuce   Lift with roots intact in the evening or early morning when the leaves are turgid. Fresh heads of uniform and attractive colour are essential. Roots should be washed and wrapped in moist tissue and inserted in a plastic bag and neatly tied. Wash upside down to avoid soil particles collecting between the leaves. Remove only markedly damaged outside leaves, and stage laid on the show bench with the firm hearts facing the front.

Marrows Young fruits of absolute uniformity and tenderness are most desirable. Aged and overripe fruits which exceed table size or approximately 15 in (38 cm) in length, dependent upon cultivar, or in the case of round cultivars 22 in (56 cm) in circumference, should be excluded. Choose specimens uniform in colour all round. Wipe clean and stage direct on to the show bench.

Onions Study the schedule carefully in order to accord with the requirements of the class. Avoid soft, stained specimens with thick, immature necks. Avoid overskinning. Uniform, well-ripened bulbs of good colour are required. Unless otherwise specified by the schedule, the tops should be tied or whipped using raffia and the roots neatly trimmed back to the basal plate. Onions are often staged on rings or soft collars. Pickling onions should not exceed 1 in (2.5 cm) in diameter.

Parsley Should be shown only by itself as a herb. It may be used as a garnish for a collection of vegetables, but should receive no points in this case except under the heading of 'arrangement'.

Parsnips Roots should be straight and of good length, evenly tapered and well developed. As with carrots, great care should be taken in lifting the roots, as bruising by fingers and scratching by soil particles will show later. Wash thoroughly with clean water.

Peas Reject specimens infested with maggots and mildew, as judges will open and check pods during their examination. When cutting from the vine retain the waxy bloom intact without finger marks. Gather by cutting with scissors and with approximately 3 in (7.5 cm) of stalk, holding the pod at all times by this. Holding pods up to a strong light will detect internal damage and reveal the number of peas in the pod. Exhibit the correct number of pods on a plate.

Potatoes Potatoes are of two classes, white and coloured, and of any shape. Select medium-sized specimens for the cultivar, generally not more than 6 oz (170 g) or tubers that lie nearly across the palm of the hand for long tubers and neatly into the palm for round tubers. Select equally matched tubers with shallow eyes. Avoid extra large tubers and those with deep set eyes. Freedom from skin blemishes which may be caused by pests, diseases or careless handling is essential. The tubers should be very carefully washed in ample, clean water with a soft sponge – on no account use a coarse cloth or brush. Stage on plates with the rose end outwards; cover with a cloth to exclude light until judging commences.

Pumpkins A single specimen of large size only need be shown.

Radishes The body of the radish should be fresh, firm, medium-sized, young, tender and brightly coloured. It should be free from blemishes and with foliage intact. Dig at the last possible moment to retain maximum turgidity. Cut spare specimens to check internal condition.

Rhubarb Stalks should be fresh, straight, long and tender with well-developed colouring. Top foliage of natural rhubarb should be cut off leaving approximately 3 in (7.5 cm) from start of leaf stalks. Foliage of forced rhubarb should not be cut off. Wipe stalks clean and trim off any bud scales at the bottom.

Salsify and Scorzonera Roots should be clean and straight and have all but the bottom 1 in (2.5 cm) of leaf stalk removed.

Shallots Stage as separate bulbs and not as clusters. Bulbs should be throughly dried, be free from staining and loose skins. Roots should be cut off to the basal plate and the tops neatly tied or whipped using raffia. Stage on dry sand or similar material which should (preferably) be of a contrasting colour and piled on the plate slightly to raise the centre. Shallots for pickling should not exceed 1 in (2.5 cm) diameter, but this is dependent upon the terms of the local show schedule.

Seakale Beet (Swiss Chard and Rhubarb Chard) Spinach and Spinach Beet Large, very fresh, thick, undamaged, well-coloured leaves are required. Defer gathering until the last possible moment to retain turgidity and so that there is as little delay as possible before staging. Leaves should be complete with a neatly trimmed stalk. Present in a flat fan shape overlapping the leaves. Careful handling is essential at all times.

Sweet Corn Confusion arises among many exhibitors at the mention that the husks and silks must be left on, yet the cobs should be shown with straight rows of grain. Exhibitors are unable to check the last named meritorious point until a husk has been removed. The following comment should clarify this point:

Fresh cylindrical cobs, fresh green husks with silks retained and not more than 1 in (2.5 cm) of stalk attached. Well set grain throughout up to the tips with straight rows of grain in an undamaged condition, of a uniform colour according to the cultivar and filled with substance of the consistency of cream. One or two husks from each cob should be pulled down, retained and neatly tucked under the cob to expose the contents of the cob.

Tomatoes Select fruit of the right shape, size and colour for the cultivar. Fruit must not be overripe or with hard 'green back' colouring around the calyx. Aim for a uniform firm set of fruit with small eye and firm, fresh calyx. Stage on plates with calyces uppermost in plate classes and with calyces downwards in collection classes.

Turnips and Swedes Select turnips for main shows of approximately the size of a cricket ball: swedes according to cultivar, but not over-large and with a small tap root. Wash carefully, remove dead foliage. Cut a spare root to check inside for disease.

SUGGESTIONS TO JUDGES

Judging is the exercise of deciding degrees of merit within agreed parameters. It is based on familiarity, knowledge and the insight gained from experience. It is most important that the criteria by which the subjects are to be judged are observed and abided by to the exclusion of all other considerations. Where a schedule is unclear or ambiguously worded a judge should consult the steward and Secretary beforehand to establish exactly what is required.

1. Personal preferences and prejudices Most people who possess the knowledge necessary for judging have some personal preferences and prejudices which they know do not find general acceptance. A judge must take care to see that he/she is not swayed by personal views. Thus a judge may be particularly fond of white flowers or have a special dislike of mauve colourings but, if so, he/she must be careful not to give undue preference to white flowers or to discount the merits of those which are mauve.

2. The opinion of the majority must prevail The judging of horticultural produce is not and never can be an exact science and a decision must often rest on something about which two opinions are tenable. When a judge believes that his/her colleagues are wrong it is his/her duty to make sure that they know his/her views but, having done that, he/she should be prepared, without any hesitation, to abide by the opinion of the majority.

3. When judges do not agree It is desirable that the group of judges for any particular class or section should be uneven in number, three being ideal. If, as is sometimes unavoidable, the number of judges is even and they are unable to agree, they should call in the referee (if there be one) or another judge or some other competent person and abide by his/her casting vote.

4. Exhibits should be judged as they are In a competitive show the time when judging will take place is always announced beforehand and is known to the competitors. Exhibits should therefore be at their best at that time and should be judged as they then are. How the exhibit probably looked some time previously or how it will probably look some time later is not relevant and a judge should put such considerations out of his/her mind.

5. Punctuality Anyone who has accepted an invitation to act as a judge should make every effort to reach the show at the time arranged. The organisers are naturally under an obligation to keep faith with exhibitors and the public in regard to the published time for the opening of the show and a judge who is late either reduces the already limited time for judging or delays the opening of the show or both.

6. Time to enter the exhibition hall   As far as possible a judge should refrain from entering the exhibition hall or tent until staging has been completed and exhibitors have left. He/she should not know to whom the various exhibits belong and it should be evident that a judge has avoided learning who the owners are.

7. Familiarity with the schedule   Before going to the show a judge should read the schedule carefully and become familiar with any special or unusual stipulations which it contains.

8. Speed in judging   Judges should devote to each class sufficient time to assess all the merits and detect all the faults in the exhibits which are 'in the running' for the prizes. Hastiness often leads to an improper decision. Thoroughness is a virtue but thoroughness and slowness are neither synonymous nor inseparable; however correct a slow judge's decision may be, if he/she unnecessarily delays the opening of the show both the organisers and the public awaiting admission will be greatly inconvenienced.

9. Should all exhibits be pointed?   It is sometimes advocated that all exhibits should be pointed. Pointing is not necessary in order to ensure that the prizes are correctly awarded, but it is often considered that by pointing all exhibits and putting with each exhibit a card showing the points awarded, the educational value of a show is increased.

It is not desirable, however, that the interval between the completion of staging and the opening of the show to the public should be longer than is necessary for proper adjudication and, except when the exhibits are few, there is usually not sufficient time to point all of them unless there are plenty of judges. It is not always practical to obtain large numbers of judges and, even when it is, sufficient competent persons are seldom available, especially during the period when most shows are held. The use of persons who are not competent may easily result in more harm than good.

Judges should never criticise inferior exhibits in public

Moreover, it should be remembered that one of the principal objects of a show is to encourage exhibitors and that it is doubtful whether those that have staged exhibits which are manifestly inferior to those that have won prizes derive much encouragement from being publicly told in detail about the shortcomings of their exhibits.

With the merits and defects of some 60 or more kinds of vegetables to be considered, a table for pointing the more common vegetables is suggested as a speedy reference guide to judges.

10. Procedure in judging a class Before assessing the merits of any exhibit in a class the judges should survey the whole class and note where the exhibits in it begin and end. Having done so they should dismiss from consideration all exhibits that are manifestly inferior and then compare the remainder. In all cases of doubt about the relative merits of exhibits they should be pointed.

When pointing an exhibit one judge should propose the number of points under each heading and any of the other judges who does not agree with that assessment should put forward his/her own opinion. As agreement is reached on each item the figure should be noted on the judging card, so that when the points for each exhibit are totalled the figure will be one on which agreement has already been reached.

11. Exhibits which appear to be of equal merit It is seldom necessary or wholly satisfactory to bracket two exhibits as equally meritorious. A careful scrutiny of exhibits which appear to be of equal merit will usually reveal something which warrants the placing of one exhibit before the other.

When there is only one award, e.g. a cup, it is essential that one exhibit should be adjudged superior to all others. If in such circumstances two exhibits obtain the same number of points, the pointing should be reviewed and, if necessary, the judges should take into consideration the arrangement of the exhibits, the relative difficulty in the cultivation of the different kinds or cultivars of which the exhibits are composed and the correctness and clearness of the labelling.

12. The withholding of prizes If the best exhibit in a class is only worthy of the second prize, the first prize should be withheld and only the second and third prizes awarded. Similarly, if after the first prize in a class has been awarded none of the remaining exhibits is worthy of the second prize, only the third prize should be awarded.

The awarding or withholding of a prize should depend solely on the merits of the exhibits irrespective of the number of entries. Should there be only one entry in a class, that should not preclude the awarding of the first prize. Although in the interests of all concerned a standard of excellence appropriate to the show should be required, when there is doubt as to whether an exhibit is worthy of the prize offered, the exhibitor should be given the benefit of the doubt, for the object of awarding prizes is to encourage.

13. Exhibits which are 'Not according to the Schedule' As the time available for judging is seldom much more than is sufficient for the judges to decide on the relative merits of the exhibits, it is recommended that one or more stewards should be appointed to ensure, as far as possible, that all exhibits are according to the schedule. But, even when stewards have been appointed, the judges are still responsible for the rejection from consideration of any exhibit which does not conform to the requirements of the schedule. The persons appointed as stewards should be competent to deal with mistakes such as too few or too many specimens and exhibits inadvertently placed in the wrong class but they cannot be expected to deal with matters which are essentially technical. The judges should write on the card of any exhibit which fails to conform to the schedule 'Not according to schedule'. A note of the way in which the exhibit fails to conform to the schedule should be added for the future guidance of the exhibitor. In *exceptional circumstances* it may be deemed preferable to advise the exhibitor privately, after the show, the reason for disqualification.

When none of the exhibits in a class is according to the schedule, the prizes offered in that class should not be awarded. But if in such circumstances the exhibits are meritorious and the non-compliance with the schedule seems to be due to a misunderstanding or to an oversight or to the schedule being imperfectly worded, the judges may recommend that 'special' prizes be awarded. The value of the prizes in such a case should be a matter for the committee to determine and may, if warranted, be the sums offered in the schedule. A disqualified exhibit cannot be eligible for consideration for 'Best in Show' but may be eligible for the award of a special prize at the discretion of the show committee.

14. Any other fruit/vegetable classes When judging 'any other' classes the pointing system should not be used as this is only intended for judging like against like. The criteria for judging given in the *Horticultural Show Handbook* should be followed, but a dish of a well grown vegetable normally receiving low points should be preferred to an indifferent dish of a vegetable or fruit normally receiving high points. The question of difficulty of cultivation should only arise when there are two outstanding exhibits, one of the 'low pointed' kind and one 'highly pointed'. In such a case the latter should be awarded the prize.

15. Uniform treatment of exhibits Judges are reminded to treat all exhibits in a uniform manner. For example, in a runner bean class at least one pod in every entry should be snapped across, not only for those entries which appear to be in the running for prizes. Omission may leave an exhibitor believing that his/her exhibit has not been judged. Everything possible must be done to give the exhibitor confidence.

It is also suggested that judges cut beetroot completely across in a slanting fashion so that any white zones or rings may be seen easily. Turnips and swedes should similarly be cut to determine the presence or absence of disease.

16. Colour in vegetables There are now many vegetables available in a range of colours, namely runner beans, dwarf French/stringless beans, beetroot, Brussels sprouts, capsicums, carrots, cucumbers, parsnips, seakale beet, Swiss chard, rhubarb chard.

Good colour for the cultivar should therefore be taken into account.

17. The pointing of certain root vegetables All the following vegetables are equally easy or difficult to grow. Some that are not so frequently grown are down-pointed. It is suggested that all receive the same total points value, i.e. 15 points:

Globe Beetroot	Salsify
Celeriac	Scorzonera
Florence Fennel	Swedes
Kohl Rabi	Turnips

THE JUDGING OF FRUITS

Assessing the merits of fruits When assessing the relative merits of dishes of any one cultivar of most fruits the following features should be considered: condition; size; colour; uniformity.

And when assessing the relative merits of single dishes of different cultivars of the same kind of fruit, quality should also be considered.

Condition Unless otherwise stated in the schedule, all fruit, except apples, pears and gooseberries should be ripe. Unless the schedule states that ripe fruit is required, apples, pears and gooseberries may be shown although not ripe. Nevertheless, where classes for apples, pears or gooseberries are included in a summer show and the schedule does not specify that the fruit must be ripe, preference should always be given to cultivars in season rather than to larger or more showy cultivars which have been picked prematurely. Over-ripeness, shrivelling (except in gages), malformations, absence of stalks or eyes, decay, cracking, blemishes due to pests or diseases, bruises or other injury due to bad packing or any other cause and imperfect bloom should be regarded as defects. The preservation of the natural bloom on the surface of fruits is greatly to be desired, not only in grapes and plums but in all fruits, including apples and pears.

Over-ripeness will be regarded as a defect in any fruit

Size All fruits, except dessert apples, should be somewhat above the average size for the cultivar but enormous specimens should not be preferred, as beyond a certain point size may become a defect, especially in dessert fruits. An exhibit of a cultivar which is naturally large should not be preferred to an exhibit of a cultivar which is naturally smaller, unless the exhibit of the larger cultivar *is equal or superior to* that of the smaller cultivar in other respects. In cooking (but not dessert) apples and in all other fruits, whether dessert or cooking, provided that the contents of two dishes are equal in all other respects, including uniformity, the dish with the larger specimens should be preferred. In grapes and currants, provided that two exhibits are equal in all other respects, including uniformity, large bunches should be preferred.

In dessert apples, it is desirable that the fruits of the average cultivar should not exceed $2^3/_4$ in (70 mm) in diameter, but the judge should be aware that some cultivars are inherently small, whereas others are naturally large, typically the triploids such as 'Jupiter' and 'Jonagold'. The judge should make due allowance for such cultivars. Nevertheless, they should not be excessively below or above the ideal size of $2^3/_4$ in (70 mm) in diameter, and it is considered the range for dessert apples should be between $2^1/_2$–3 in (62–75 mm) in diameter. Examples of inherently small or large dessert apples are:

Small 'Margil', 'Merton Charm', 'Pitmaston Pineapple', 'Pixie', 'Sunset' and 'Winston'.

Large 'Belle de Boskoop', 'Blenheim Orange', 'Charles Ross', 'Crispin', 'Gascoyne's Scarlet', 'Herring's Pippin', 'Jonagold', 'Jupiter', 'King of Tompkins County', 'Reinette du Canada', 'Rival', and 'Wealthy'.

Colour Attractive, naturally-produced colour is meritorious but colour resulting from the removal of natural bloom or any form of polishing should be regarded as defective in any fruit. An exhibit of a cultivar which is of inferior quality but naturally highly coloured should not be preferred to an exhibit of a cultivar of superior quality which naturally does not have a very attractive colour (e.g. Peach 'Alexandra Noblesse') unless the less highly-coloured exhibit is inferior in some other respect.

Uniformity All the specimens exhibited on a dish should be uniform i.e. alike in size, form and colour.

Maximum points for a dish The exhibition value of any kind of fruit is governed by the difficulty of producing a perfect dish. The maximum points for a perfect dish (irrespective of quality) will be as follows:

	Maximum Points		Maximum Points
Apples, Cooking	16	Citrus fruits	16
Apples, Dessert	20	Currants, Black	12
Apricots	12	Currants, Red and White	8
Blackberries	8	Currant × Gooseberry Hybrids	8
Blueberries	8	Damsons	8
Bullaces	8	Figs	12
Cherries, Sweet and Sour	12	Gooseberries	12

	Maximum Points		*Maximum Points*
Grapes grown outdoors	16	Kiwi Fruits	12
Grapes grown under glass		Medlars	5
other than those		Melons	20
mentioned below	20	Nectarines	20
'Cannon Hall'	24	Nuts including Walnuts	8
'Muscat of Alexandria'	24	Peaches	20
'Madresfield Court'	22	Pears, Cooking	14
'Mrs Pearson'	22	Pears, Dessert	20
'Mrs Pince'	22	Pineapples	20
'Muscat Hamburgh'	22	Plums, Cooking	12
'Prince of Wales'	22	Plums, Dessert	16
Hybrid Berries, e.g.		Quinces	8
Loganberries, Nectarberries,		Raspberries	12
Boysenberries, Tayberries		Strawberries	16
and Japanese Wineberries	8		

In assessing the relative merits of different cultivars of the same kind of fruit, consideration may be given to the allocation of additional points for 'quality', which is the term to denote superior flavour, texture and juiciness.

Alphabetical List of Fruits

Apples, Cooking

Meritorious Large, shapely, solid fruits with eyes and stalks intact and clear unblemished skins of a colour characteristic of the cultivar.

Defective Fruits that are small, mis-shapen, over-ripe or soft or that have damaged eyes or lack stalks or have any blemish, including evidence of any physiological disorder such as bitter-pit or glassiness.

Condition	5 points
Size	6 points
Uniformity	5 points
Total	**16 points**

Apples, Dessert

Meritorious Optimum-sized shapely fruits with eyes and stalks intact and clear unblemished skins of the natural colour characteristic of the cultivar.

Defective Fruits that are too small or too large, mis-shapen, over-ripe or soft or that have damaged eyes or lack stalks or are not well coloured, or have any blemish, including evidence of any physiological disorder such as bitter-pit or glassiness.

Condition	6 points
Suitability of size	4 points
Colour	4 points
Uniformity	6 points
Total	**20 points**

Apricots

Meritorious Large, highly-coloured, clear-skinned, ripe fruits free from any blemish.

Defective Fruits that are small or poorly coloured or that lack stalks or clear skins or that are unripe or over-ripe or have any blemish.

Condition	3 points
Size	3 points
Colour	3 points
Uniformity	3 points
Total	**12 points**

Blackberries and Hybrid Cane Fruits
including Loganberries, Tayberries, Boysenberries, Nectarberries, Sunberries & Japanese Wineberries

Meritorious Large, ripe fruits, of good colour, free from blemishes, in good condition and having stalks.

Defective Fruits that are small, unripe or over-ripe, of a dull colour, not in good condition or that have blemishes due to insect damage or imperfect fertilisation or lack stalks.

Condition	2 points
Size	2 points
Shape	2 points
uniformity	2 points
Total	**8 points**

Blueberries

Meritorious Large, ripe fruits of good colour and bloom, free from blemishes, in good condition, shown as stalked bunches.

Defective Fruits that are small, unripe or over-ripe, of a dull colour, not in good condition, blemished or with imperfect bloom, shown singly or as incomplete, stalkless bunches.

Condition	 4	points
Size	 2	points
Uniformity	 2	points
Total	 8	**points**

Boysenberries

See Blackberries

Bullaces

Meritorious Large, ripe but firm fruits, of good colour, with perfect bloom and having stalks.

Defective Fruits that are small, unripe or so ripe as to be soft, of poor colour or that have imperfect bloom or lack stalks.

Condition	 2	points
Size	 2	points
Colour	 2	points
Uniformity	 2	points
Total	 8	**points**

Cherries, Sweet and Sour

Meritorious Large, ripe fruits, of brilliant colour, with unshrivelled stalks.

Defective Fruits that are small, unripe or over-ripe, of dull colour or that are splitting or have any blemish or that lack stalks or have shrivelled stalks.

Condition	 3	points
Size	 3	points
Colour	 3	points
Uniformity	 3	points
Total	 12	**points**

Citrus Fruits

Meritorious Large, shapely ripe fruits, without stalks, of good even colour natural to the cultivar with bright, shiny unblemished skins.

Defective Fruits that are small, mis-shapen, unripe or over-ripe of dull or uneven colour or have any blemish.

Condition	4 points
Size	4 points
Colour	4 points
Uniformity	4 points
Total	**16 points**

Currants, Black

Meritorious Strigs with full complement of berries. Berries large, ripe and of a uniform, bright, jet-black colour. Stalks fresh.

Defective Strigs without full complement of berries. Berries small, unripe or over-ripe or unevenly ripened or of a dull colour or having shrivelled stalks.

Condition	3 points
Size	3 points
Colour	3 points
Uniformity	3 points
Total	**12 points**

Currants, Red and White

Meritorious Strigs with full complement of berries. Berries large, ripe and of a uniform, brilliant colour. Stalks fresh.

Defective Strigs without full complement of berries. Berries small, unripe or over-ripe or unevenly ripened or of a dull colour or having shrivelled stalks.

Condition and colour	4 points
Size	2 points
Uniformity	2 points
Total	**8 points**

Currant x Gooseberry Hybrids
including Jostaberry and Worcesterberry

Meritorious Strigs with full complement of berries. Berries large, ripe, uniform and of even colour. Stalks fresh.

Defective Strigs without full complement of berries. Berries small, unripe or over-ripe, of poor or uneven colour, diseased or blemished or having shrivelled stalks.

Condition and colour	4	points
Size	2	points
Uniformity	2	points
Total	**8**	**points**

Damsons

Meritorious Large, ripe but firm fruits, of good colour, carrying perfect bloom and having stalks.

Defective Fruits small, unripe or so ripe as to be soft, of poor colour or with imperfect bloom or lacking stalks.

Condition	2	points
Size	2	points
Colour	2	points
Uniformity	2	points
Total	**8**	**points**

Figs

Meritorious Large, fully ripe fruits, of good colour with bloom and stalks intact.

Defective Fruits small, unripe, of poor colour or with imperfect bloom. Splitting is not a fault.

Condition	4	points
Size	4	points
Colour	2	points
Uniformity	2	points
Total	**12**	**points**

Gooseberries

Meritorious Large, ripe or unripe fruits as appropriate for the season, uniform and unblemished, of good colour, complete with stalks.

Defective Fruits small, uneven, over-ripe, diseased, blemished, of poor colour or lacking stalks.

Condition	.4 points
Size	.3 points
Colour	.2 points
Uniformity	.3 points
Total	**12 points**

Grapes (Glasshouse dessert)

Meritorious Large bunches, although large bunches of a poor quality are not so meritorious as smaller ones of a good quality. Symmetrical, complete, well balanced bunches, of uniform size and shape and properly thinned so that each berry has had room to develop. Large berries, of uniform size, good colour, fully ripe and well finished with a dense, intact bloom.
Note: In grapes quality is allowed for in the ordinary maximum points in the table.

Defective Bunches that are small, ill balanced, lacking uniformity in size or shape or are loose or so crowded that some berries have not had room to develop properly. Berries that are small, lacking in uniformity, of poor colour or not fully ripe and poorly finished or over-ripe, diseased or that have little or only imperfect bloom or have shanked or have spots or blemishes of any sort.

Condition	.5 points
Size, shape and density of bunch	5 points
Size and uniformity of berry . .	5 points
Colour	.5 points
Total	**20 points**

If the cultivar is either 'Muscat of Alexandria' or 'Cannon Hall', add 4 points.

If the cultivar is either 'Muscat Hamburgh', 'Madresfield Court', 'Mrs Pearson', 'Mrs Pince' or 'Prince of Wales', add 2 points.

Grapes grown out-of-doors for wine or dessert

Meritorious Large, complete, well filled and balanced bunches carrying large berries, unblemished, typical of the cultivar, of uniform size, good colour, fully ripe and well finished with a dense intact bloom.

Defective Bunches that are small, under-developed, lacking uniformity, blemished, rotting, split, have shanked, unripe or over-ripe, poorly finished or with little or imperfect bloom.

Condition 4	points
Size, shape and density of bunch 4	points
Size and uniformity of berry . 4	points
Colour 4	points
Total **16**	**points**

Japanese Wineberries

See Blackberries, page 52

Kiwi Fruits (Chinese gooseberries)

Meritorious Large fruits, evenly shaped and uniform, with unblemished skins and stalks intact.

Defective Fruits that are small or are uneven, lack uniformity or have any blemish or are without stalks.

Condition 4	points
Size 4	points
Uniformity 4	points
Total **12**	**points**

Loganberries

See Blackberries, page 52

Medlars

Meritorious Large fruits with clean skins and stalks intact.

Defective Fruits that are small or have blotched skins.

Condition 1	point
Size 2	points
Uniformity 2	points
Total **5**	**points**

Melons

Meritorious A large fruit (for the cultivar), clean, shapely, free from blemishes, fully ripe and well finished.

Defective A small fruit (for the cultivar), or one that is unripe or over-ripe or is blemished or mis-shapen.

Condition	7	points
Appearance	7	points
Size	6	points
Total	. . . . **20**	**points**

Nectarberries

See Blackberries, page 52

Nectarines

See Peaches and Nectarines, below

Nuts, including Walnuts

Meritorious Large nuts with clean shells and plump kernels filling the cavities. In walnuts, nuts that are well-sealed with thin shells.

Defective Nuts that are small, or have spotted shells or shrivelled kernels or kernels that do not fill the shells or are unsound. In walnuts, nuts that are poorly sealed or have shells that are not thin.

Condition	2	points
Size, including uniformity	. .6	points
Total	. . . .**8**	**points**

Peaches and Nectarines

Meritorious Large fruits (for the cultivar), fully ripe with the colour natural to the cultivar well developed, free from bruises and other blemishes.

Defective Fruits that are small (for the cultivar), unripe or over-ripe with colour not well developed or that are bruised or have split stones or any other blemish.

Condition	5	points
Size	5	points
Colour	5	points
Uniformity	5	points
Total	. . . . **20**	**points**

Pears, Cooking

Meritorious Large, shapely fruits with eyes and stalks intact and clear, unblemished skins of a colour characteristic of the cultivar.

Defective Fruits that are small, mis-shapen, over-ripe or soft or that have damaged eyes or lack stalks or have any blemish.

Condition	4 points
Size	6 points
Uniformity	4 points
Total	**14 points**

Pears, Dessert

Meritorious Large for the cultivar, shapely fruits with eyes and stalks intact and clear, unblemished skins of the natural colour characteristic of the cultivar.

Defective Fruits that are small, mis-shapen or shrivelled or that have damaged eyes or lack stalks or are not well coloured or have any blemish.

Condition	6 points
Size	4 points
Colour	4 points
Uniformity	6 points
Total	**20 points**

Pineapples

Meritorious A fruit that is large for the cultivar, ripe and of a golden colour throughout, shapely, with segments of even size, free from blemish and having a fresh-looking crown that is in proportion to the fruit, i.e. about half its length.

Defective A fruit that is small for the cultivar, not fully ripe or over-ripe, of uneven shape, having poorly formed segments due to imperfect fertilisation, showing insect damage, having a crown that is not fresh or is not in proportion to the fruit.

Condition	10 points
Size	6 points
Form	4 points
Total	**20 points**

Plums, Cooking

Meritorious Large, firm, ripe fruits, of good colour, carrying perfect bloom, and having stalks.

Defective Fruits that are small, unripe or so ripe as to be soft, of poor colour or with imperfect bloom or lacking stalks.

Condition	3 points
Size	3 points
Colour	3 points
Uniformity	3 points
Total	**12 points**

Plums, Dessert

Meritorious Large fully ripe fruits, of good colour, with bloom intact and having stalks.

Defective Fruits that are small, unripe or over-ripe, of poor colour, with imperfect bloom or lacking stalks. Slight shrivelling in gages and some other plums need not be considered a defect.

Condition	5 points
Size	3 points
Colour	4 points
Uniformity	4 points
Total	**16 points**

Quinces

Meritorious Large, shapely fruits with eyes and stalks intact and unblemished skins.

Defective Fruits that are small or mis-shapen or have damaged eyes or lack stalks or have any blemish.

Condition	3 points
Size	2 points
Uniformity	3 points
Total	**8 points**

Raspberries

Meritorious Large, ripe fruits, of good colour, free from blemishes, in good condition and having stalks.

Defective Fruits that are small, unripe or over-ripe, of a dull colour, not in good condition or have blemishes due to insect damage or imperfect fertilisation or that lack stalks.

Condition	4 points
Size	3 points
Colour	3 points
Uniformity	2 points
Total	**12 points**

Strawberries

Meritorious Large, ripe fruits, of good colour, bright and fresh, free from blemish, in good condition and having stalks.

Defective Fruits that are small, unripe or over-ripe, of a dull colour, not in good condition or that are 'hard-nosed' through imperfect fertilisation or lacking stalks.

Condition	4 points
Size	4 points
Colour	4 points
Uniformity	4 points
Total	**16 points**

Tayberries

See Blackberries, page 52

THE JUDGING OF VEGETABLES

Assessing the merits of vegetables In assessing the merits of exhibits of vegetables the following features should usually be considered: condition; size; uniformity.

Condition Cleanliness, freshness, tenderness and presence or absence of coarseness and blemishes.

Size This is meritorious if accompanied by quality (but only in those circumstances) as the production of large specimens of good quality requires more skill than the production of small specimens. The size of vegetable most suitable for table use varies with the consumer.

Uniformity The state of being alike in size, shape and colour.

Maximum points for a dish The exhibition value of any kind of vegetable is governed by the difficulty of producing a perfect dish. The maximum points for a perfect dish will be as follows:

	Maximum Points		Maximum Points
Artichokes, Chinese	10	Cabbages, Red	15
Artichokes, Globe	15	Cabbages, Savoy	15
Artichokes, Jerusalem	10	Calabrese	15
Asparagus	15	Capsicums (Sweet Peppers) and Chili Peppers	15
Asparagus Pea, Mangetout and Petit Pois	12	Carrots, long	20
Aubergines	18	Carrots, other than long	18
Beans, Broad	15	Cauliflowers, including White Heading 'Broccoli'	20
Beans, Climbing, other than Runner	15	Celeriac	15
Beans, Dwarf French/ Stringless	15	Celery, American green	18
		Celery, self-blanching	18
Beans, Runner and Stringless Runner	18	Celery, trench	20
		Chicory, Heads (Chicons)	15
Beetroot, Globe and Cylindrical	15	Chives	10
Beetroot, long	18	Corn Salad (Lambs' Lettuce)	10
Broccoli, Sprouting and Coloured-headed	15	Courgettes	10
		Couve Tronchuda	12
Brussels Sprouts	15	Cress	10
Cabbages, Chinese	15	Cress, American or Land	10
Cabbages, Green	15	Cucumbers, House or Frame	18

	Maximum Points		Maximum Points
Cucumbers, Ridge and Outdoor	15	Parsnips	20
Dandelion, Blanched	10	Peas	20
Endive	15	Potatoes	20
Fennel, Florence	15	Pumpkins	10
Garlic	12	Radishes	10
Herbs	5	Rhubarb, Forced	15
Kales	12	Rhubarb, Natural	12
Kohl Rabi	12	Salading Vegetables, Miscellaneous	10
Leaf Lettuce	10	Salsify	15
Leeks (Blanch and Intermediate)	20	Scorzonera	15
Leeks (Pot)	20	Seakale	15
Lettuces	15	Seakale Beet	12
Marrows, including Squashes	15	Shallots, Exhibition	18
		Shallots, Pickling	12
Mushrooms	15	Spinach	12
Mustard or Rape	10	Spinach, New Zealand	12
Okra	18	Spinach Beet	12
Onions	20	Swedes	15
Onions under 8 oz	15	Sweet Corn	15
Onions, Pickling	10	Tomatoes	20
Onions, Green Salad	10	Turnips	15
		Watercress	10

Alphabetical List of Vegetables

Artichokes, Chinese

Meritorious Long, clear skinned, plump tubers.

Defective Small, thin, shrivelled tubers.

Condition	 4	points
Size and shape	 4	points
Uniformity	 2	points
Total	. . . . **10**	**points**

Artichokes, Globe

Meritorious Large, heavy, shapely (rounded or conical), well-closed heads of plump, fleshy scales.

Defective Heads that are small, light in weight, irregular or loose or that have thin or shrivelled scales.

Condition including solidity	5 points
Size and shape	4 points
Colour	3 points
Uniformity	3 points
Total	**15 points**

Artichokes, Jerusalem

Meritorious Shapely, large tubers with smooth, clear skins.

Defective Tubers of very irregular shape or small or that have rough or patchy skins.

Condition	4 points
Size and shape	4 points
Uniformity	2 points
Total	**10 points**

Asparagus

Meritorious Long, straight, thick, plump, bright stems with well-closed scales.

Defective Stems that are short, crooked, thin, shrivelled or dull-coloured or that have open scales.

Condition	5 points
Size, shape and colour	5 points
Uniformity	5 points
Total	**15 points**

Asparagus Pea
including Petit Pois and Mangetout

Meritorious Well shaped pods typical of the cultivar, about 2 in (5 cm) long

Defective Mis-shapen pods that are obviously under or over developed.

Condition including colour	. 5 points
Size of pods	. 4 points
Uniformity	. 3 points
Total	**12 points**

Aubergines

Meritorious Large, shapely, solid, bright, well-coloured fruits free from blemishes.

Defective Fruits that are small, mis-shapen, hollow, shrivelled, dull or poorly coloured.

Condition	. 5 points
Size and shape	. 5 points
Colour	. 4 points
Uniformity	. 4 points
Total	**18 points**

Beans, Broad

Meritorious Large, fresh, well-filled pods with clear skins and tender seeds. Size according to cultivar.

Defective Pods that are small, not fresh or imperfectly filled or that have spotted skins or contain seeds that are not tender.

Condition	. 5 points
Size and shape	. 4 points
Colour	. 3 points
Uniformity	. 3 points
Total	**15 points**

Beans, Climbing, other than Runner

See Beans, Dwarf French/Stringless, page 66

Beans, Dwarf French/Stringless

Meritorious Straight, fresh, tender snap pods with stalks and of even length and good, green colour with no outward sign of seeds.

Defective Pods that are mis-shapen, dull, shrivelled, tough or stringy or that have prominent seeds.

Condition and freshness. . . .	. 5 points
Size and shape	. 4 points
Colour	. 3 points
Uniformity	. 3 points
Total	**15 points**

Beans, Runner and Stringless Runner

Meritorious Long, slender, straight, fresh pods of good colour with no outward sign of seeds.

Defective Pods that are short, broad, mis-shapen, tough or stringy, of poor shape and colour or that have prominent seeds.

Condition	. 5 points
Size and shape	. 5 points
Colour	. 4 points
Uniformity	. 4 points
Total	**18 points**

Beetroot

Meritorious Beetroot of the long type: broad, clean shoulders, evenly tapered; of the globe type: spherical with small tap roots; of either type: good sized roots of not more than tennis-ball size, fangless with smooth clear skins and flesh of a uniform dark colour.

Defective Roots that are mis-shapen, fangy or tough or have rough skins or flesh that is ringed or of a pale colour.

Beetroot, Globe and Cylindrical

Condition	. 5 points
Colour of flesh	. 5 points
Uniformity	. 5 points
Total	**15 points**

Beetroot, Long

Condition	. 5	points
Size and shape	. 4	points
Colour of flesh	. 5	points
Uniformity	. 4	points
Total	**18**	**points**

Broccoli, Sprouting and Coloured-headed

See also Calabrese, page 68

The vegetables which fall under this heading should be judged on a maximum of 15 points. The types are numerous and varied and their merits and defects cannot be briefly summarised. They must therefore be left to the discretion of the judges in the rare case where a schedule contains a class for any of these types or where they appear in the 'Any Other Vegetable' classes.

Condition including solidity	. 5	points
Colour	. 5	points
Size and uniformity	. 5	points
Total	**15**	**points**

Brussels Sprouts

Meritorious Fresh, solid, tightly closed sprouts of good colour. Size according to cultivar.

Defective Sprouts that lack freshness, good colour, solidity or are not tightly closed.

Condition including solidity	. 5	points
Size and colour	. 5	points
Uniformity	. 5	points
Total	**15**	**points**

Cabbages, Chinese

Meritorious Fresh, firm, solid heads, outside leaves a fresh green colour, free from pest damage.

Defective Soft, loose heads that lack freshness or are damaged by pests.

Condition including solidity	. 5	points
Colour and firmness	. 5	points
Uniformity	. 5	points
Total	**15**	**points**

Cabbages, Green

Meritorious Shapely, fresh and solid hearts with the surrounding leaves perfect and bloom intact and of good colour. Size according to cultivar with approximately 3 in (7.5 cm) of stalk, pointed or round cultivars.

Defective Hearts that are soft, split or tough or lack freshness or are pest-damaged.

Condition including solidity	. 5	points
Size and shape	4	points
Colour	3	points
Uniformity	3	points
Total	**15**	**points**

Cabbages, Red

Meritorious Solid heads, well-coloured, shapely, fresh, with bloom intact and free from blemish. Size and condition according to cultivar.

Defective Heads that are small, loose, split, poorly coloured lacking in bloom or pest-damaged.

Condition including solidity	. 5	points
Size and shape	4	points
Colour	3	points
Uniformity	3	points
Total	**15**	**points**

Cabbages, Savoy
& other hybrid types

See Cabbages, Green, above

Calabrese

Meritorious Fresh, solid, tightly closed heads of good colour.

Defective Heads that lack freshness and are irregularly shaped, lacking in solidity, of poor colour and that are not tightly closed or with evidence of flowering.

Condition including solidity	. 5	points
Size and shape	4	points
Colour	3	points
Uniformity	3	points
Total	**15**	**points**

Capsicums (Sweet Peppers) and Chili Peppers

Meritorious Fresh, brightly coloured green, red or yellow fruits with colour according to cultivar.

Defective Fruits that are dull, shrivelled or poorly coloured.

Condition	5	points
Size and shape	4	points
Colour	3	points
Uniformity	3	points
Total	**15**	**points**

Carrots, Long/Other than Long

Meritorious Tender roots of good shape, colour and size according to cultivar, free from side roots; skins clean and bright for both long and other than long.

Defective Roots that are coarse and mis-shapen, fangy, dull or poorly coloured, green at the crown or pest-damaged.

	Long			Other than Long	
Condition	6	points		5	points
Size and Shape	4	points		4	points
Colour	5	points		5	points
Uniformity	5	points		4	points
Total	**20**	**points**		**18**	**points**

Cauliflowers
including Winter Cauliflower (White Heading 'Broccoli')

Meritorious Heads with symmetrical, close, solid, white curds, free from stain or frothiness. Size according to cultivar.

Defective Heads of irregular shape, beginning to open, yellowing or stained or showing leaf in the curd.

Condition including solidity	5	points
Colour	5	points
Size and shape	5	points
Uniformity	5	points
Total	**20**	**points**

Celeriac

Meritorious Roots smooth and globe shaped. Size according to cultivar.

Defective Roots that are rough, fanged or flat.

Condition including solidity . . 5	points
Size and shape 5	points
Uniformity 5	points
Total **15**	**points**

Celery

Meritorious Large, firm but crisp, brittle and free from stringiness with fresh, clean and undamaged leaves.

Defective Heads that are small or coarse or loose or have visible flower-stems or have thin, soft, pithy, stringy, imperfectly blanched, blemished or pest-damaged leaf-stalks or diseased foliage and evidence of embryo flower stems.

	Trench	Self-blanching	American green
Condition including firmness & crispness	5 points	5 points	5 points
Size and shape	5 points	5 points	5 points
Colour (blanch)	5 points	4 points	4 points
Uniformity	5 points	4 points	4 points
Total	**20 points**	**18 points**	**18 points**

Chicory, Heads (Chicons)

Meritorious Long, solid, crisp, tender and well-blanched heads.

Defective Heads that are open, soft, loose, limp, tough or badly blanched.

Condition 5	points
Size and shape 4	points
Colour (Blanch) 3	points
Uniformity 3	points
Total **15**	**points**

Chives

See Salading Vegetables, Miscellaneous, page 80

Corn Salad or Lambs' Lettuce

See Salading Vegetables, Miscellaneous, page 80

Courgettes

Meritorious Young, tender, shapely fruits, 4 to 6 in (10-15 cm) in length, of any colour but well matched.

Defective Fruits that are not young or tender or that are over-length, mis-shapen or ill-matched.

Condition	4 points
Colour	4 points
Uniformity	2 points
Total	**10 points**

Couve Tronchuda

See Seakale Beet, page 81

Cress

See Salading Vegetables, Miscellaneous, page 80

Cress, American or Land

See Salading Vegetables, Miscellaneous, page 80

Cucumbers

Meritorious Fresh, young, green, tender, straight fruits of uniform thickness with short handles and with flowers still adhering.

Defective Fruits that are old, yellowing, crooked, soft, of irregular thickness with long handles or lacking flowers.

	House and Frame	Ridge and outdoor grown
Condition	5 points	5 points
Size and shape	5 points	4 points
Colour (blanch)	4 points	3 points
Uniformity	4 points	3 points
Total	**18 points**	**15 points**

Dandelion, Blanched

See Salading Vegetables, Miscellaneous, page 80

Endive

Meritorious Well-formed, well-blanched, crisp, tender heads, free from pest-damage.

Defective Heads that are poorly developed, imperfectly blanched, limp, tough, or pest-damaged.

Condition	. 5	points
Colour (blanch)	. 3	points
Size	. 4	points
Uniformity	. 3	points
Total	**15**	**points**

Fennel

See Herbs, page 73

Fennel, Florence

Meritorious Large, solid base stems, free from coarseness or visible flower stems, having clean leaf-stalks.

Defective Stems that are small at the base, coarse or loose or that have imperfect leaf-stalks or visible flower stems.

Condition and solidity	. 5	points
Size and shape	. 4	points
Colour	. 3	points
Uniformity	. 3	points
Total	**15**	**points**

Garlic

Meritorious Round, solid, well-ripened bulbs with thin necks. Garlic displayed for exhibition should not be divided into segments (cloves).

Defective Bulbs that are asymmetrical, soft, poorly ripened or that have thick necks.

Condition	. 3	points
Size	. 2	points
Colour	. 3	points
Uniformity	. 4	points
Total	**12**	**points**

Herbs

Meritorious Fresh, healthy, clean foliage.

Defective Material that is not fresh and clean, is yellowing or showing other signs of age or pest damage or has any disease such as mint rust or parsley leaf-spot.

Condition	. . . . 2 points
Colour	. . . . 2 points
Size	. . . . 1 points
Total	. . . . **5 points**

Kales

Meritorious Fresh, sturdy, well-developed heads.

Defective Heads that are limp, drawn or poorly developed.

Condition	. . . . 5 points
Size	. . . . 2 points
Colour	. . . . 3 points
Uniformity	. . . . 2 points
Total	. . . . **12 points**

Kohl Rabi

Meritorious Fresh, tender, small-leaved 'bulbs', not larger than about billiard ball size (ie approximately about 2 in (5 cm) in diameter), free from injury.

Defective Bulbs that are old, tough or gross or have coarse foliage, or that are cracked or have injury of any sort.

Condition	. . . . 5 points
Size	. . . . 3 points
Shape	. . . . 2 points
Uniformity	. . . . 2 points
Total	. . . . **12 points**

Leaf Lettuce

See Salading Vegetables, Miscellaneous, page 80

Leeks (Blanch and Intermediate)

(see note on page 135)

Meritorious Solid, thick, long-shafted, well-blanched leeks, tight--collared with clean, spotless skins and no tendency to bulbing.

Defective Leeks that are soft, thin, tapering, short-shafted, imperfect-ly blanched, discoloured or bulbous.

Condition	. 8 points
Solidity	. 4 points
Colour (blanch)	. 3 points
Uniformity	. 5 points
Total	**20 points**

Leeks (Pot)

(see note on page 135)

Meritorious Firm, solid heavy leeks with unbroken, clean and un-blemished skins. Well blanched not greater than 6 in (15cm) to the tight button. Uniformity of size, straightness of barrel and colour of foliage.

Defective Soft, thin, split buttons, too long-shafted, evidence of seed heads, disease, damage and malformation.

Condition	. 8 points
Solidity	. 4 points
Colour (blanch)	. 3 points
Uniformity	. 5 points
Total	**20 points**

Note: The National Pot Leek Society give additional points for vol-ume or cubic capacity measured on volume of blanched shaft to tight 6 in (15 cm) button (i.e. from basal plate to lowest unbroken leaf, including the veil where present and around the barrel). One point for every 10 cu in (164 cm^3) and decimal point for part of 10 to a present maximum of 20 points or 200 cu in (3277 cm^3). Tables for the calculation of cubic capacity are obtainable from the Secretary of the National Pot Leek Society.

Lettuces

Meritorious Firm, tender, unbroken hearts of good colour.

Defective Hearts that are soft or tough or show signs of bolting or have outer leaves that are limp or of poor colour or are showing signs of pest damage.

Condition	5 points
Solidity and texture	4 points
Colour	3 points
Uniformity	3 points
Total	**15 points**

Marjoram

See Herbs, page 73

Marrows
including Squashes and other Edible Cucurbits

Meritorious For marrows specifically, young, tender fruits of absolute uniformity are essential. Stage directly on the bench.

Defective Fruits that are not young or tender or that are mis-shapen or ill-matched. Aged and over-ripe marrows or fruits that exceed 15 in (38 cm) in length, or in the case of round fruited cultivars 22 in (56 cm) in circumference, should be rigorously excluded.

Condition including tenderness	5	points
Size, shape and colour	5	points
Uniformity	5	points
Total	**15**	**points**

Mint

See Herbs, page 73

Mushrooms

Stage of development should be stated in the Schedule i.e. 'Button', 'Closed Cap' or 'Open Cap'.

Meritorious Mushrooms that are plump, rounded, with unbroken edges and free from blemishes. If the gills are visible they should be pinkish or pinkish brown.

Defective Mushrooms that show any signs of shrivelling or are flattened or have broken edges or any blemish or have blackening gills.

Condition and freshness . . . 5	points
Firmness and colour of cap	
and gills 5	points
Uniformity 5	points
Total **15**	**points**

Mustard or Rape

See Salading Vegetables, Miscellaneous, page 80

Okra

Meritorious Fresh, slender pointed fruits, 6 to 8 in long (15 to 20 cm) free from blemishes.

Defective Fruits that are mis-shapen, shrivelled, dull or poorly coloured.

Condition 5	points
Size 5	points
Colour 4	points
Uniformity 4	points
Total **18**	**points**

Onions

Meritorious Firm, thin-necked bulbs. At autumn and winter shows the bulbs must be well-ripened. In summer show as grown. Size and shape according to cultivar.

Defective Bulbs that are small or soft or have soft or thick necks or have broken outer skins or have been skinned excessively.

Condition 5	points
Size 5	points
Shape and colour 5	points
Uniformity 5	points
Total **20**	**points**

Onions under 8 oz (227 g)

Condition	6	points
Size, shape and colour	4	points
Uniformity	5	points
Total	**15**	**points**

Onions, Pickling

Meritorious Small, very firm, well-ripened uniform bulbs not exceeding 1 in (2.5cm) in diameter.

Defective Large, soft or poorly ripened bulbs.

Condition	3	points
Size	3	points
Shape and colour	2	points
Uniformity	2	points
Total	**10**	**points**

Onions, Green Salad

Meritorious Fresh young plants, showing no tendency to bulb and having white bases.

Defective Plants that have leaves that are yellow-tipped or have been cut; or plants that are too large or are bulbous or have bases other than white.

Condition	3	points
Size	3	points
Colour	2	points
Uniformity	2	points
Total	**10**	**points**

Parsley

See Herbs, page 73

Parsnips

Meritorious Well-developed, well-shouldered, shapely, smooth-skinned, white roots, free from side roots or blemishes.

Defective Roots that are under-sized or lack good shoulders or are mis-shapen or have rough, discoloured skins, side roots, blemishes or canker.

Condition	6 points
Size and Shape	5 points
Colour	4 points
Uniformity	5 points
Total	**20 points**

Peas

Meritorious Large, fresh pods of a deep green with bloom intact, free from disease or pest damage and well filled with tender seeds. Colour according to cultivar with waxy bloom intact.

Defective Pods that are small, not fresh or of poor colour or having very imperfect bloom or are diseased or pest damaged or poorly filled or containing seeds that are old or maggoty.

Condition	7 points
Fullness & size of pod	5 points
Colour	3 points
Uniformity	5 points
Total	**20 points**

Peppers, Sweet

See Capsicums, page 69

Potatoes

Meritorious Medium-sized of about 6 oz (170 g) per tuber; shapely, clean, clear-skinned tubers; eyes few and shallow.

Defective Tubers that are very small or very large or are mis-shapen or have damaged, speckled or patchy skins or have many or deep eyes.

Condition	5 points
Size	3 points
Shape	4 points
Eyes	3 points
Uniformity	5 points
Total	**20 points**

Pumpkins

Meritorious A shapely, large, firm fruit of even colour and ripeness.

Defective A fruit that is mis-shapen, soft, unevenly ripened or with spotted or marked skin.

Condition	5 points
Size and solidity	5 points
Total	**10 points**

Radishes (Winter)

Meritorious Fresh, medium sized, good coloured roots free from blemishes.

Defective Roots tough, spongy, of a dull colour or blemished.

Condition	3 points
Size	3 points
Colour	2 points
Uniformity	2 points
Total	**10 points**

Radishes (other than Winter Radishes)

Meritorious Fresh, medium-sized, young, tender, brightly-coloured roots, free from blemishes and having short, intact foliage.

Defective Roots that are not fresh or are very small or large, old, tough, spongy, of a dull colour or blemished in any way or have flower-stems showing or have long or trimmed foliage.

Condition	3 points
Size	3 points
Colour	2 points
Uniformity	2 points
Total	**10 points**

Rhubarb, Forced

Meritorious Fresh, straight, thick, brightly coloured stalks with un-developed leaf-blades.

Defective Stalks that are limp, crooked, thin or dull-coloured or have developed leaf-blades or have had leaf-blades removed.

Condition	4 points
Colour	4 points
Straightness and length	4 points
Uniformity	3 points
Total	**15 points**

Rhubarb, Natural

Meritorious Fresh, straight, long, tender stalks with well-developed red colouring with leaf blades trimmed back to approximately 3 in (7.5 cm).

Defective Stalks that are limp, crooked, stunted, tough or lacking in red colouring.

Condition	.3 points
Length and thickness	.3 points
Colour	.3 points
Uniformity	.3 points
Total	**12 points**

Sage

See Herbs, page 73

Salading Vegetables, Miscellaneous

See page 137 (i.e. other than those dealt with separately)

Meritorious Material that is young, fresh, clean and of attractive appearance.

Defective Material that is not young or is limp or gritty or at all unattractive.

Condition	.4 points
Size	.2 points
Colour	.2 points
Uniformity	.2 points
Total	**10 points**

Salsify

Meritorious Large, shapely, evenly tapering, clean, smooth-skinned roots, free from side roots.

Defective Roots that are small, mis-shaped or taper unevenly or are fangy or lack a clean, smooth skin.

Condition	.4 points
Size and shape	.4 points
Colour	.3 points
Uniformity	.4 points
Total	**15 points**

Savory, Summer and Winter

See Herbs, page 73

Scorzonera

Meritorious Large, shapely, clean, smooth-skinned roots, of a good dark colour, free from side roots.

Defective Roots that are small, mis-shapen or fangy or pale or lack a clean smooth skin.

Condition	4 points
Size and shape	4 points
Colour	3 points
Uniformity	4 points
Total	**15 points**

Seakale

Meritorious Stout, crisp, well-blanched heads with leaf-blades undeveloped.

Defective Heads that are spindly, limp or poorly blanched or that have developed leaf-blades.

Condition and solidity . .	5 points
Size and colour (Blanch) . .	4 points
Freedom from leaf-development	3 points
Uniformity	3 points
Total	**15 points**

Seakale Beet
including Rhubarb Chard and Couve Tronchuda

Meritorious Fresh, long, broad, thick, solid, white leaf-stalks with dark green leaves, of good colour for the cultivar.

Defective Leaf-stalks that are limp, short, narrow, thin or not white.

Condition	5 points
Size	3 points
Colour	2 points
Uniformity	2 points
Total	**12 points**

Shallots, Exhibition

Meritorious Firm, well-ripened, shapely bulbs with thin neck and of good size and colour. Necks to be whipped or tied with raffia.

Defective Bulbs that are asymmetrical or soft or that have thick necks or are poorly ripened.

Condition	.7 points
Size and shape	.4 points
Colour	.2 points
Uniformity	.5 points
Total	**18 points**

Shallots, Pickling

Meritorious Round, solid, well-ripened bulbs of good colour with thin necks. Bulbs for pickling should not exceed 1 in (2.5 cm) in diameter. Necks whipped or tied with raffia.

Defective Bulbs that are asymmetrical or soft or that have thick necks or are poorly ripened.

Condition	.4 points
Size and shape	.4 points
Colour	.2 points
Uniformity	.2 points
Total	**12 points**

Spinach

Meritorious Large, thick, fresh, undamaged, dark-green leaves.

Defective Leaves that are small, thin, limp, broken, pale green or yellowing.

Condition	.4 points
Size and substance	.3 points
Colour	.3 points
Uniformity	.2 points
Total	**12 points**

Spinach, New Zealand

Meritorious Large, fresh, dark-green tips about pencil thickness and approximately 3 in (7.5 cm) long.

Defective Small, rusty or yellowing tips.

Condition	4 points
Size and substance	3 points
Colour	3 points
Uniformity	2 points
Total	**12 points**

Spinach Beet

Meritorious Large, thick, fresh, undamaged, dark-green leaves.

Defective Leaves that are small, thin, limp, broken, pale green or yellowing.

Condition	4 points
Size and substance	3 points
Colour	3 points
Uniformity	2 points
Total	**12 points**

Swedes

See Turnips and Swedes, page 84

Sweet Corn

Meritorious Fresh, cylindrical cobs, well set throughout including the tips, with straight rows of undamaged grains, fresh green husks and silks attached. Grain that is in the best condition for table use and of a uniform colour, which may be pale cream, white or an intermediate colour.

Defective Cobs that are not fresh or are unduly tapered or have irregular rows of grain or are badly set or have husks that are shrivelled and straw coloured or without silks. Grains that are starchy, watery or doughy or have anthers between them or are not of a uniform colour.

Condition	5 points
Size and set of grain	5 points
Colour	2 points
Uniformity	3 points
Total	**15 points**

Sweet Peppers

See Capsicums, page 69

Tarragon

See Herbs, page 73

Thyme

See Herbs, page 73

Tomatoes

Meritorious Medium-sized (approximately $2^1/_2$ in or 70 mm in diameter), of about 5 or 6 fruits to the pound, ripe but firm, richly coloured fruits with calyces attached. Good shape and size for the cultivar.

Defective Fruits that are small or very large or of uneven shape or unripe or over-ripe or of a dull colour or green-backed or that lack the calyces.

Condition	.5 points
Colour	.5 points
Size and shape	.5 points
Uniformity	.5 points
Total	**20 points**

Turnips and Swedes

Meritorious Turnips: about the size of a cricket ball; Swedes: medium-sized. Clear-skinned, solid, shapely roots with small tap-roots, and no side roots. The flesh of turnips may be white or yellow.

Defective Roots that are very small or very large or have patchy skins or are spongy or of irregular shape or have large tap-roots or side roots or are affected by brown heart or disease.

Condition	.5 points
Size and shape	.3 points
Colour	.3 points
Uniformity	.4 points
Total	**15 points**

Watercress

See Salading Vegetables, Miscellaneous, page 80

THE JUDGING OF FLOWERS AND ORNAMENTAL PLANTS

In assessing the merits of most exhibits of flowers and some exhibits of pot plants consideration should be given to condition and uniformity.

Condition An exhibit is in good 'condition' when the material of which it consists is in the most perfect stage of its possible beauty and is fresh and free from damage due to weather, pests, diseases, faulty handling or any other cause.

Uniformity An exhibit is 'uniform' when items of which it consists are alike in age, size and form.

The way in which an exhibit of flowers or ornamental plants is staged is naturally particularly important. But in the following scales no points are allocated to 'arrangement' because, although attractive presentation will automatically influence the judges, the extent to which it should and will do so depends not so much on the kind of flower or plant as on the nature of the exhibit for which the schedule calls, e.g. a single bloom or a vase of many blooms. In all cases, however, an exhibit that is arranged in such a way as to display the merits of the flowers or plants to best advantage will inevitably and rightly make a more favourable impression on the judges, even though the flowers or plants in the two exhibits may be of equal merit.

Annual, Biennial, Bulbous and Herbaceous Plants
in Flower

(other than those for which separate criteria are given on pages 88 to 121)

Vases of one species/cultivar

Meritorious Good fresh condition. A good proportion (70%) of flowers fully developed and appropriately positioned on their stem(s). The petals should be properly positioned on the flowers and of a shape, texture and colour typical of the species or cultivar. The foliage should be clean, healthy and undamaged by weather or pests. Stems should be typical of the species or cultivar and, in the case of flowers that bloom in spikes such as larkspurs and hyacinths or in 'crowns' such as hippeastrums and crown imperials, should be straight and firm right to the tip with the flowers evenly spaced and the open florets touching or almost touching one another.

Defective Poor condition. Some flowers either undeveloped or past their peak. Petals unnaturally twisted or mis-shapen or of poor texture or colour for the species or cultivar. Foliage or flowers that are mud-splashed, or showing signs of insect or fungal damage. Stems that are untypically short, twisted weak or bent.

Condition of flowers and stems	6 points
Shape and texture of flowers and foliage	6 points
Colour	4 points
Uniformity	4 points
Total	**20 points**

Note: For show purposes, the ornamental bracts surrounding the flowers of plants such as *Euphorbia, Salvia sclarea* (clary) and *Salvia horminum* are considered to be a part of the flower and the plant may be judged as 'in bloom' if these are fully expanded even though the true flowers are not completely open.

Mixed vases

The above criteria may be applied equally as well to vases of mixed flowers from different genera, species or cultivars, i.e. not less than three different plants, but the judging criteria should be adjusted as follows:

Condition and quality of flowers, foliage and stems	8 points
Colour, texture and arrangement	6 points
Symmetry and balance of exhibit (presentation) . . .	6 points
Total	**20 points**

Ornamental Trees and Shrubs
in flower or fruit (including seedheads)

(other than those for which separate criteria are given on pages 88 to 121)

Vases of one species/cultivar

Meritorious Good fresh condition. A good proportion (70%) of flowers or fruits fully developed and well positioned on shapely, well balanced sprays, stems or branches. Individual flowers or fruits well shaped and of a texture, size and colour typical of the species or cultivar. Fresh, healthy, clean, undamaged foliage of good colour and of a size and pattern typical of the species or cultivar.

Defective Poor, limp or starved condition. Flowers or fruits that are mis-shapen, undeveloped or past their best or sparsely distributed. Sprays, stems or branches that are unevenly developed, unnaturally twisted or stunted or not typical of the species or cultivar. Foliage that shows signs of damage by insects, weather or disease or is under- or over-sized for the species or cultivar.

Condition of flowers/fruit and foliage	5 points
Shape and texture of flowers, fruit and foliage	5 points
Colour	4 points
Stems/sprays/branches	3 points
Balance or symmetry of the exhibit	3 points
Total	**20 points**

Note: For show purposes, the ornamental bracts surrounding the flowers of plants such as *Cornus kousa*, *Davidia* and *Euphorbia* are considered to be a part of the flower and the plant may be judged as 'in bloom' if these are fully expanded even though the true flowers are not completely open.

Mixed vases

The above criteria may be applied equally as well to vases of mixed sprays from different genera, species or cultivars i.e. not less than three different plants, but the judging criteria should be adjusted as follows:

Condition and quality	8 points
Colour, texture and arrangement	6 points
Symmetry and balance of exhibit (presentation)	6 points
Total	**20 points**

Alpine-house and Rock-garden Plants

Meritorious A plant of a size suitable for an alpine house or rock garden and hardy enough to survive an average winter in a frost-free house. (It need not be a native of mountainous regions and may be a perennial herbaceous plant, an annual or a shrub.) Other things being equal, preference should be given to a plant which is difficult to grow. A plant 'in character' (i.e. its character in nature). Many perfect open blooms in a plant grown for its flower. Closeness and firmness in a cushion plant. Rarity (i.e. in cultivation). A conifer or a shrub on its own roots should be preferred to a grafted specimen with the exception of certain genera, such as *Pinus,* that are usually propagated by grafting. Colourful foliage in a plant grown for the colour of its leaves.

Defective A plant that attains too great a size to be suitable for an alpine house or rock garden or that is not hardy enough to survive an average winter in an unheated house. A plant that is common in cultivation or easy to grow if in competition with one that is rare in cultivation or difficult to grow. A plant that does not conform to its character in nature. A plant that is grown for its flowers but has few flowers or flowers that are not open or are past their best. A cushion plant that is loose or patchy. A conifer or shrub that has been grafted, with the exception of certain genera, such as *Pinus,* that are usually propagated by grafting, or have been clipped or artificially dwarfed. A plant grown for its coloured foliage but lacking colour.

Suitability	. 2 points
Rarity in cultivation	. 2 points
In character	. 2 points
Cultivation	. 4 points
Total	**10 points**

Auriculas, Alpine

Meritorious Foliage, stem, pedicels and pip as in Show auriculas. A circular tube, filled by the anthers, hiding the stigma. A golden, yellow, cream or white centre, without farina (a mealy coating). A richly coloured but not necessarily dark edge, without trace of coarseness, shaded to a paler tint.

Defective Foliage, stem, pedicels and pip as in Show Auriculas. A tube that is irregular or showing the stigma. An edge that is not richly coloured.

Foliage, stem and pedicels	. 8 points
Pips	. 4 points
Tube	. 2 points
Centre	. 3 points
Edge	. 3 points
Total	**20 points**

Auriculas, Double

Meritorious Well-balanced and healthy foliage. A strong stem suffi-ciently long to bear the truss well above the foliage, arising from a single rosette. A truss carried on pedicels of a length that avoids any overcrowding and rigid enough to prevent the pips from drooping. The pips should be of rich or clear colours. Doubling to be symmetrical and to fill the corolla effectively. All pips should possess the same degree of doubling.

Defective Foliage that is ill-balanced, limp or unhealthy. A stem that is weak or short. Pedicels that allow the pips to be over-crowded or to droop. Pips that are not of rich or clear colours. Doubling that is asymmetrical or lacking effect or possessing a defect whereby the doubling shows a marked decrease from the earliest to the latest pip.

Foliage, stem and pedicels . . 7	points
Colour of pips 4	points
Doubling - symmetry and effect 6	points
Doubling - degree 3	points
Total **20**	**points**

Auriculas, Show

Meritorious Well-balanced, healthy foliage. A strong stem, sufficiently long to bear the truss well above the foliage, arising from a single rosette. A truss consisting of not fewer than five fully developed pips (three in a seedling) carried on pedicels sufficiently long to avoid overlapping of the pips. A perfectly flat, round, smooth-edged pip consisting of lobes without notches or serrations. A circular tube with a diameter approximately equal to one-sixth of the diameter of the pip, slightly raised at the edge of the paste (inner circular zone of the petals, surrounding the central tube), of a deep yellow colour and filled by the anthers, hiding the stigma. A pure white, smooth paste, free from crack or blemish, circular in outline and of a width equal to that of the ground-colour and edge together. A dense ground-colour, forming a perfect circle near the paste, the darker and richer the colour the better, though red should not be regarded as a fault. A bright green, grey or white edge of about the same width as the ground-colour. In 'selfs' the colour should be uniform throughout and without shading. The paste should be as required in the edged section and should be about equal in width to that of the border colour.

Defective Foliage that is ill-balanced, limp or unhealthy. A stem that is weak or short. A truss that has fewer than five well-developed pips (fewer than three in a seedling) or has pedicels that are too short to prevent overlapping of the pips. A pip that is not flat, circular or smooth-edged or has fewer than six lobes or has notched or serrated lobes. A tube that is irregular or has a diameter exceeding one-sixth of that of the pip or is pale-coloured or has a visible stigma. A paste (inner circular zone of the petals, surrounding the central tube) that is not pure white or is rough, cracked or blemished or lacks a circular outline or is of a width that is not approximately equal to that of the combined ground-colour and edge. A ground-colour that does not have a perfectly circular outline or is wider than half the width of the paste or that lacks density or richness. An edge that is not self-coloured or that is wider than half the width of the paste.

Scale for Show auriculas other than 'selfs':

Foliage, stem and pedicels	. 7 points
Pips	. 2 points
Tube	. 2 points
Paste	. 3 points
Ground-colour	. 3 points
Edge	. 3 points
Total	**20 points**

Scale for 'selfs'

Foliage, stem and pedicels	. 7 points
Pips	. 2 points
Tube	. 3 points
Paste	. 4 points
Border	. 4 points
Total	**20 points**

Begonias, Double Tuberous

Meritorious A well-balanced plant, bearing flowers in size and number proportionate to the size of the plant and to the cultivar where known. Large flowers of good substance, circular in outline with broad overlapping petals culminating in one centre. Colour decided and clear. In picotee cultivars the colours should not 'run' one into another. Foliage that is clean, healthy and undamaged. Stems that are stout and erect.

Defective An ill-balanced plant, carrying flowers that are few or small for the size of the plant or the cultivar where known. Small flowers, of poor texture or irregular outline or having divided centres. Long, narrow petals. Pale or damaged or spotted foliage. Spindly, weak stems.

Plant	. 5 points
Stems	. 3 points
Form of flower	. 6 points
Colour	. 3 points
Foliage	. 3 points
Total	**20 points**

Bonsai

A bonsai is essentially a tree encouraged to conform in all respects with an ordinary tree, except for its miniature size. Natural dwarf trees are not bonsai, unless trained to look like a large natural tree in shape and restricted to a size smaller than their own maximum potential. A bonsai and its container must together present a satisfactory, well-balanced and aesthetic unity.

Meritorious A strong, well-shaped trunk tapering upwards, merging naturally with the growing medium. Surface roots fanning out from the base of the trunk and gradually disappearing into the soil. Well-proportioned head of branches well-spaced and set on the trunk and without scars or marks of training. A tree looking as natural as possible in its surroundings. Pots, preferable in monochrome glaze, in proportion to the tree. Polychrome pots are permissible but are best used for non-flowering and non-fruiting specimens. Tree so placed in the pot as to create a visual balance. Flowers, fruit and foliage in proportion to the size of tree. Trees planted well raised in the pot, so that the bole can be seen clearly over the rim of the pot when viewed at eye level.

Defective Weak, badly shaped trunks or those that look like sticks or branches stuck in the ground. Badly spaced, cut, scarred or crossed branches. Noticeable artificial training; uncharacteristic growth for species. Snagged or abruptly cut roots visible above the soil or dead fibrous roots standing in the air. Trees out of balance. Flowers, fruit or foliage out of proportion to the size of the tree. Soil surface and bole of trunk sunk well below the rim of the pot. Unnecessary additional ornaments or decoration.

Cacti and Succulents

Meritorious A large specimen for the species or form, well-balanced, in good health, free from injury of any sort including damaged spines or defective 'bloom'. Other things being equal, a plant that is in flower will be preferred to one that is not. A species or form that is rare in cultivation will be preferred to one that is common.

Defective A specimen that is small for the species or form, is in poor health or has any injury, damaged spines or defective 'bloom'. A specimen that is not in flower or is of a species or form common in cultivation, if in competition with one that is in flower or is rare.

Condition	8 points
Difficulty of cultivation . .	4 points
Conformity to type	4 points
Rarity	4 points
Total	**20 points**

Carnations, Border (including Picotees)

Border Carnations may be classed according to colour as follows:

Selfs, which must be of one clear colour.

Fancies, which must have a clear ground-colour and be marked or suffused by a contrasting colour or colours.

Picotees, which must have a clear ground-colour, with an even, unbroken margin of contrasting colour around every petal.

Fancies and Picotees may be further divided according to their ground-colour. Cloves may be any colour or colours, but must possess a strong clove scent.

Meritorious Good condition. Flowers that are fresh, symmetrical and circular in outline. Firm petals with smooth edges, slight fimbriation permitted. Guard-petals that are large, broad, smooth and carried at right-angles to the calyx. Inner petals that lie regularly and smoothly over the guard-petals, though the centre petals may stand up somewhat and form a crown. Calyx should be unbroken. Strong stems. Colour or colours clear, bright and well defined. A strong scent. Uniformity.

Defective Unsatisfactory condition. Flowers that are small or not circular in outline. Petals that lack substance or have serrated edges or show a marked tendency to incurve or are so numerous as to appear crowded. Guard-petals that are small, narrow or are incurved or recurved. Calyx split or requiring bands. Stems that are weak. Lack of uniformity. Unless specifically permitted by the schedule, exhibits with stem supports or calyx bands should be disqualified.

Form (of flower)	7 points
Freshness	7 points
Colour	3 points
Size	3 points
Total	**20 points**

Carnations, Perpetual-flowering

Perpetual-flowering Carnations may be classed according to colour as follows:

Selfs, which must be of one clear colour.

Fancies, which must have a clear ground-colour and be marked or suffused with a contrasting colour or colours. Fancies may be further divided according to their ground-colour.

Meritorious Good condition. Flowers that are large, symmetrical, circular in outline and have full centres. Guard-petals that are flat, firm and well formed. (The edges may be either smooth or regularly serrated.) Calyx unbroken. Strong stems proportionate in length and thickness to the size of the flowers. Clear and bright colours. A strong scent. Uniformity.

Defective Unsatisfactory condition. Flowers that are small or asymmetrical. Calyx split or requiring bands. Weak, clumsy or short stems. Lack of scent. Lack of uniformity. Unless specifically permitted by the schedule, exhibits with stem supports or calyx bands should be disqualified.points

Form (of flower)	7	points
Freshness	7	points
Colour	3	points
Size	3	points
Total	**20**	**points**

Chrysanthemums

The following paragraphs contain advice about judging most of the different sections into which chrysanthemum cultivars have been classified.

Classification

Late-Flowering (Indoor Cultivars)

Section	1	Large Exhibition (Incurving and Reflexing)
"	2	Medium Exhibition
"	3	Exhibition Incurved
"	4	Reflexed Decoratives
"	5	Intermediate Decoratives
"	6	Anemones
"	7	Singles
"	8	Pompons
"	9	Sprays
"	10	Spidery, Plumed and Feathery
"	11	Any other types

October-Flowering

Section	13	Incurved Decoratives
"	14	Reflexed Decoratives
"	15	Intermediate Decoratives
"	16	Large October-flowering
"	17	Singles, October-flowering
"	18	Pompons, October-flowering
"	19	Sprays, October-flowering
"	20	Any other types, October-flowering

Early-Flowering (Outdoor Cultivars)

Section	23	Incurved Decoratives
"	24	Reflexed Decoratives

Section	25	Intermediate Decoratives
"	26	Anemones
"	27	Singles
"	28	Pompons
"	29	Sprays
"	30	Any other types

Cultivars in sections 13 to 20 (October-flowering types) may normally be shown in classes at shows for early-flowering types but those in sections 13 to 16 may also usually be shown in classes at shows for late-flowering types. Early-flowering chrysanthemums (sections 23 to 30) include all cultivars that in a normal season bloom in the open ground before October 1. Though these blooms must be grown in the open it is usually permissible to protect them from weather damage.

Section 1

Meritorious **Reflexing types**: a bloom in which the breadth and depth are approximately equal and that has good shoulders and a full centre. Florets (which may be either flat and broad or quilled) gracefully reflexed, of good substance, fresh to the tips, unspotted and of bright colour. **Incurving types**: a bloom that is globular or nearly so, with a full centre. Florets that are broad, incurved (either closely and regularly or loosely and irregularly), fresh to the tips and of bright colour.

Defective A bloom that is much broader than deep or lacks good shoulders, is coarse or has a depressed centre. Florets that are not gracefully reflexed, are of poor substance, stale (no longer fresh) at the tips, spotted or of dull colour or drooping.

Note: Cups may be used to support the blooms but they must not exceed 3 in (7.5 cm) in diameter.

Points See page 97

Section 2

Meritorious As in Section 1.

Defective As in Section 1.

Points See page 97

Sections 3, 13 and 23

Meritorious A bloom that is compact and globular or nearly so. Florets that are broad, smooth, rounded at the tips, of sufficient length to form a graceful curve, closely and regularly arranged, firm, fresh (including the outer ones) and of a clear, decisive colour.

Defective A bloom that is loose, flat, has a hollow centre or is irregular in outline. Florets that are narrow, loosely or irregularly arranged, soft, lacking freshness or of dull or undecided colour.

Note: No cups or rings are permissible but, in Section 3, the stem may be supported.

Points See page 97

Sections 4, 14 and 24

Meritorious Blooms that are broad and deep and have full centres. Florets of good substance, bright in colour and fresh to the tips. Florets that reflex gracefully and overlap one another perfectly. In types with quilled, sharply pointed florets that stand out stiffly, freshness to the tips is of particular importance.

Defective Blooms that are narrow or shallow or lack full centres or have daisy-eyes, i.e. visible disc-florets. Florets that are of poor substance, stale, drooping, dull in colour, ragged or misplaced.

Points See page 97

Section 5, 15 and 25

Meritorious Blooms that are globular in outline, with breadth and depth approximately equal. Florets that are broad, incurving (either closely and regularly or loosely and irregularly), of good substance, fresh to the tips and of bright colour. In semi-reflexing types, a pleasing contrast in colour between the outer reflexing and the inner recurving florets.

Defective Blooms that are too broad for their depth and not globular in outline or have hollow centres. Florets that are narrow, of poor substance, stale or of dull colour.

Points See page 97

Sections 6, 16 and 26

Meritorious Blooms that have fresh, deep, symmetrical 'cushions' (i.e. discs) of even size and bright colour. Ray-florets that are fresh and of bright colour: either broad to the tips, flat and of equal length or pointed and of uneven size.

Defective Blooms with cushions that are stale, shallow, malformed, of uneven size or dull colour. Ray-florets that are drooping or not fresh to the tips or of a dull colour.

Points See page 97

Sections 7, 17 and 27
Blooms with approximately five rows of ray-florets though medium-sized blooms may have more than five rows.

Meritorious Flowers borne at right angles to the stems. Ray-florets that are broad, flat, of good substance, fresh to the tips and of a bright colour. Disc-florets that are fresh, clear and regular.

Defective Flowers that are not borne at right angles to the stems. Ray-florets in excess or that are narrow, incurving or not flat or are of poor substance, drooping or stale. Disc-florets that are old, dull or irregular. Slight reflexing or incurving at the tips of ray-florets should be regarded as defective in some cultivars.

Points See page 97

Sections 8, 18 and 28

Meritorious Blooms that are symmetrical (ball-shaped), with full centres, of uniform size and bright colour.

Defective Blooms that are asymmetrical, lack full centres, are of uneven size or of a dull colour.

Points See page 97

Sections 9, 19 and 29
A spray for the purposes of these sections is the last flowering growth consisting of one stem (not a branch) with or without a central flower or bud.

Meritorious The blooms of sprays should be fresh, clean, of uniform size, development and colour. Individual blooms evenly spaced and not overlapping one another. Foliage small, fresh and clean.

Defective Dead or faded blooms, colour variation and poor foliage.

Points See page 97

Scales of Points

Section 1

Form	 5	points
Size	 6	points
Freshness and firmness of florets	6	points
Colour and Staging	 3	points
Total	. . . . **20**	**points**

Sections 3, 13 and 23

Form	 6	points
Size	 5	points
Freshness and firmness of florets	5	points
Colour	 2	points
Foliage and Staging	. . . 2	points
Total	. . . . **20**	**points**

All other sections

Form	 5	points
Size (according to classification)	5	points
Freshness and firmness of florets	5	points
Colour	 3	points
Foliage and Staging	. . . 2	points
Total	. . . . **20**	**points**

For shows organised by the National Chrysanthemum Society or for chrysanthemum classes in shows organised by societies affiliated to the NCS, the use of the NCS scale of points may be obligatory. Details of these scales may be obtained from the Secretary of the National Chrysanthemum Society.

Chrysanthemums, Specimen Plants in Pots

Meritorious A symmetrical plant, 'facing all round', with a single main stem for not less than 1 in (2.5 cm) between the soil and the first branch or break. Blooms numerous and of high quality. Foliage ample, clean and healthy. Stems that have been bent gradually from near their bases. Supports and ties inconspicuous. There should be not less than 18 in (45 cm) of clear stem between soil level and the bottom of the head in standard Pompons and not less than 24 in (60 cm) in standards of large-flowered cultivars.

Defective A plant that is not symmetrical or faces only one way or has more than one main stem immediately above the soil. Blooms that are not sufficiently numerous for the size of the plant or are lacking in quality. Stems that have been bent abruptly. Supports or ties that are obtrusive or ties too near the blooms.

Number, quality and freshness of blooms	. . 10	points
Foliage	. 4	points
Training	. 6	points
Total	**20**	**points**

Chrysanthemums, Cascade

Meritorious A well-trained and balanced plant, evenly furnished with fully open blooms that are fresh and bright in colour. Training frames, canes and ties should be as inconspicuous as possible.

Defective A badly trained, unevenly balanced plant with few blooms open or with blooms past their best and fading. Training frames, canes and ties that are conspicuous or badly positioned.

Number, quality and freshness of blooms	. . 8	points
Foliage	. 2	points
Training	10	points
Total	**20**	**points**

Chrysanthemums, Charm

Meritorious A symmetrical plant 'facing all round', evenly furnished with fully open blooms that are fresh and bright in colour. Foliage clean and healthy. Plant size commensurate with the size of the pot.

Defective A plant that is not symmetrical or faces only one way, or is unevenly furnished with a low proportion of open blooms, or having flowers that are faded and dull. A loose open plant.

Number, quality and freshness of blooms	. . 10	points
Foliage	. 4	points
Training	. 6	points
Total	**20**	**points**

Daffodils (Narcissi)

Meritorious   Flower carried at nearly a right angle to the stem, except in species and hybrids where a pendent flower is typical, e.g. *Narcissus triandrus* and its hybrids. Perianth of smooth texture and good substance. Segments broad and overlapping from the base for a good proportion of their length, flat or slightly twisted symmetrically in each segment or in alternate segments. Corona or crown of good colour, texture and substance, proportionate to the perianth in length and width, any frill or flange at the brim being even and uniform. Stem straight and strong and proportionate in length to the size of the flower. Neck of flower short. In double cultivars, segments and colour symmetrically arranged.

Defective   (N.B. These defects would not necessarily apply to species.)   A flower that faces downwards, except in species and hybrids in which a pendent flower is typical. A perianth of poor or uneven colour, ribbed, thin or hooded. Segments that are too narrow to overlap for a good proportion of their length or that are neither flat nor symmetrically twisted, or that have notches, nicks or tears. A corona or crown of poor colour, texture or substance or that has a frill or flange that is uneven or has spots at the margin. A stem that is weak or bent and disproportionate in length to the flower. A long neck. In double cultivars, segments or colour unevenly distributed.

In a class for single blooms:

Condition	4 points
Form	4 points
Colour	4 points
Size (for the cultivar)	3 points
Texture	3 points
Poise	3 points
Stem	2 points
Presentation	2 points
Total	**25 points**

In a class with three or more blooms to a vase:

Condition	4 points
Form	4 points
Colour	4 points
Size (for the cultivar)	3 points
Texture	3 points
Poise	3 points
Stems	2 points
Uniformity	3 points
Presentation	4 points
Total	**30 points**

The following classification of daffodils has been adopted by The Royal Horticultural Society,

Division 1 Trumpet Daffodils of Garden Origin
Distinguishing characters: One flower to a stem; corona (trumpet) as long as or longer than the perianth segments (petals).

Division 2 Large-cupped Daffodils of Garden Origin
Distinguishing characters: One flower to a stem; corona (cup) more than one-third, but less than equal to the length of the perianth segments (petals).

Division 3 Small-cupped Daffodils of Garden Origin
Distinguishing characters: One flower to a stem; corona (cup) not more than one-third the length of the perianth segments (petals).

Division 4 Double Daffodils of Garden Origin
Distinguishing characters: One or more flowers to a stem, with doubling of the perianth segments or the corona or both.

Division 5 Triandrus Daffodils of Garden Origin
Distinguishing characters: Characteristics of *N. triandrus* clearly evident: usually two or more pendent flowers to a stem; perianth segments reflexed.

Division 6 Cyclamineus Daffodils of Garden Origin
Distinguishing characters: Characteristics of *N. cyclamineus* clearly evident: usually one flower to a stem; perianth segments reflexed; flower at an acute angle to the stem, with a very short pedicel (neck).

Division 7 Jonquilla Daffodils of Garden Origin
Distinguishing characters: Characteristics of the *N. jonquilla* group clearly evident: usually one to three flowers to a rounded stem; leaves narrow, dark green; perianth segments spreading, not reflexed; flowers fragrant.

Division 8 Tazetta Daffodils of Garden Origin
Distinguishing characters: Characteristics of the *N. tazetta* group clearly evident: usually three to twenty flowers to a stout stem; leaves broad; perianth segments spreading, not reflexed; flowers fragrant.

Division 9 Poeticus Daffodils of Garden Origin
Distinguishing characters: Characteristics of the *N. poeticus* group without admixture of any other; usually one flower to a stem;

perianth segments pure white; corona usually disc-shaped, with a green or yellow centre and a red rim; flowers fragrant.

Division 10　Species, Wild Variants and Wild Hybrids
All species and wild or reputedly wild variants and hybrids, including those with double flowers.

Division 11　Split-corona Daffodils of Garden Origin
Corona split rather than lobed and usually for more than half its length.

Division 12　Miscellaneous Daffodils
All daffodils not falling into any one of the foregoing Divisions.

Note: The characteristics for Divisions 5 to 9 are given for guidance only; they are not all necessarily expected to be present in every cultivar assigned thereto.

Dahlias

Classification

Group	1	Single flowered	Group	6	Ball
"	2	Anemone-flowered	"	7	Pompon
"	3	Collarette	"	8	Cactus
"	4	Waterlily-flowered	"	9	Semi-cactus
"	5	Decorative	"	10	Miscellaneous

Note: Since 1973, the National Dahlia Society has sub-divided Groups 5, 8 and 9 for show purposes, as follows:

Giant	over 260 mm	(10.2 in)
Large	220–260 mm	(8.6–10.2 in)
Medium	170–220 mm	(6.7–8.6 in)
Small	115–170 mm	(4.5–6.7 in)
Miniature	up to 115 mm	(4.5 in)

Group 6 is sub-divided for show purposes as follows:

Small Ball	115–170 mm	(4.5–6.7 in)
Miniature Ball	up to 115 mm	(4.5 in)

Group 7 (Pompons) must not exceed 52 mm (2 in) in diameter.

Meritorious
The following standards may be used when judging the different categories:

Double-flowered Dahlia (other than Ball and Pompon dahlias)
Bloom symmetrical and outline perfectly circular. A firm, circular, closed centre, proportionate to the size of the flower. Bloom fresh

and clean, all florets intact, firm and without blemish or defect. Colour or colours clear and well-defined and either consistent or evenly shaded or tipped throughout the bloom. Bloom 'full', having, without over-crowding, sufficient florets to prevent gaps in formation and outline and to give depth to the bloom, which should be approximately two-thirds, or more, of the diameter. Bloom (other than pompons) poised at an angle of not less than 45 degrees to the stem, which should be straight and of a length and thickness proportionate to the size of the bloom.

Ball Dahlias

Blooms should be ball-shaped but the tendency towards flatness on the face of the larger cultivars is acceptable. Ray-florets (blunt or rounded at the tips, with margins spirally arranged and involute for more than half their length) small, proportionate to the size of the bloom, radiating evenly from the centre; symmetrically arranged, dressing back to the stem to complete the ball shape of the bloom. Florets compact and dense at the centre. Bloom fresh and clean, all florets intact, firm and without blemish or defect. Colour or colours clear and well-defined and either consistent or evenly shaded or tipped throughout the bloom. Bloom poised at an angle of not less than 45 degrees to the stem, which should be straight and of a length and thickness proportionate to the size of the bloom.

Pompon Dahlias

Bloom perfectly globular, not exceeding 52 mm (2 in) in diameter (for show purposes). Florets involute for the whole of their length, evenly and symmetrically arranged throughout the bloom and dressing back fully to the stem. Central florets compact, dense at the centre and slightly convex. Bloom fresh and clean, all florets intact, firm and without blemish or defect. Colour or colours clear and well-defined and either consistent or evenly shaded throughout the bloom. Bloom facing upwards on a straight, firm stem.

Single and Collarette (Collerette) Dahlias

Eight or more outer florets, possibly overlapping but not assuming double formation, equal in size, uniform in shape and formation, radiating evenly and regularly away from the central disc in a single flat plane with the outer edges rounded or pointed. Inner florets or collar of collarettes uniform in size, symmetrical and approximately half the length of the outer florets, even in colour and formation. Central disc flat and circular, containing not more than two rows of pollen-bearing stamens. Bloom fresh and clean, all florets intact, firm and without blemish or defect. Colour or colours clear and well-defined and either consistent or evenly shaded or tipped throughout the bloom. Bloom poised at an angle of 45 degrees to the stem, which should be straight and proportionate to the size of the bloom.

Waterlily Dahlias

Blooms should be fully double and the face view circular in outline and regular in arrangement. A firm, circular, closed centre, proportionate to the size of the flower. The depth of the bloom should be approximately half the diameter. Bloom should be poised at an angle of not less than 45 degrees to the stem, which should be straight and of a length and thickness proportionate to the size of the bloom.

Anemone-flowered Dahlias

Close and compact group of tubular florets comprising the centre of the bloom, circular in outline. Outer ray-florets equal in size, uniform in shape and formation, generally flat and regularly arranged around the central florets. Bloom fresh and clean, all florets intact, firm and without blemish or defect. Colour or colours clear and well-defined and either consistent or evenly shaded or tipped throughout the bloom. Bloom poised at an angle of 45 degrees to the stem, which should be straight and proportionate to the size of the bloom.

Miscellaneous Dahlias

Bloom fresh and clean and all florets intact, firm and without blemish. Colour or colours clear and well-defined and either consistent or evenly shaded or tipped throughout the bloom. Bloom poised at an angle of not less than 45 degrees to the stem, which should be straight and proportionate to the size and formation.

Exhibits

An exhibit of dahlias should be so arranged that all the blooms face in the same direction, are clear of each other and a pleasant and balanced effect is achieved. Blooms should be staged with some dahlia foliage, preferably on the stem. The foliage should be clean, healthy and undamaged. The names of all cultivars in an exhibit should be clearly stated.

Defective As a general principle anything that detracts from the perfection of a bloom, or an exhibit, is a 'fault' and the seriousness or otherwise of the fault depends upon the degree of imperfection. In judging an exhibit the following faults should be evaluated accordingly.

It is a very serious fault if a bloom is malformed, faces downwards, has been badly damaged, has limp drooping florets, has had a large number of florets removed, has an open (daisy-eyed) centre (double flowered cultivars only), has a centre that is hard and green, large and undeveloped or badly distorted, or has a gap created by a missing outer floret (this refers to Groups 1-4 only).

The following faults may be either minor or serious, in accordance with the amount by which the fault detracts from the perfection of a bloom. Quality: an oval, sunken or isolated centre, irregular or oval outline of bloom, uneven, irregular, or unbalanced formation, florets lacking freshness or bleached, discoloured, faded, eaten, bruised, malformed or otherwise blemished, where florets have been removed, stems that are bent, weak, short-jointed, thick or out of proportion, uneven or inconsistent colouring, uneven tipping of bi-coloured blooms, shallow blooms, i.e. those lacking depth or fullness and blooms that are either immature or past their best.

Angle of Bloom (pompon): the bloom of a pompon should face upwards on a straight, firm stem and any variation of this should be regarded as a fault.

Exhibits must be disqualified for any of the following reasons: 1. Blooms exceeding the recommended maximum sizes given in the classification. 2. Blooms artificially supported above the top level of the vase. 3. Incorrect number of blooms in an exhibit. 4. Classified blooms exhibited in wrong class. If a vase in a multi-vase exhibit be NAS then the whole exhibit must be disqualified. While the whole exhibit cannot be considered for an award, awards to individual vases, other than the disqualified vases, are permitted (e.g. best vase in its group in that exhibit).

The foregoing paragraphs were prepared in consultation with the National Dahlia Society. Rules for the disqualification of dahlia exhibits for oversize have been introduced by the National Dahlia Society for use in their own shows and details are obtainable from the Secretary of the NDS. The NDS does not favour the use of a scale of points for judging. The Royal Horticultural Society considers that in certain cases such a scale may provide a useful guide and the following scale is accordingly suggested for use if desired.

Form and centre	. . . . . .	5	points
Condition	. . . .	10	points
Stem	. . . .	3	points
Colour	. . . .	2	points
Total	. . . .	**20**	**points**

Delphiniums

In judging delphiniums no differentiation should be made between spikes shown with or without laterals.

Meritorious Good condition. Long, tapering, straight spikes, length in keeping with type (short, medium or tall), symmetrical and well filled with flowers but not overcrowded. Large circular flowers, with broad petals of good substance and colour. No faded or fallen petals. The 'bee' or centre should be clear and distinct whether of self or contrasting colour or striped. Seed pods inconspicuous. Clean, healthy, fresh and undamaged foliage.

Defective Unsatisfactory condition. Spikes that are short relative to type or crooked or malformed in any way or that are sparsely or irregularly furnished with flowers or overcrowded. Flowers that are small or have petals that are narrow or lacking in substance or that have faded or fallen petals. Signs of stripped or removed flowers. Conspicuous seed pods. Foliage that is damaged, withered or unhealthy.

Condition	5 points
Form of spike	5 points
Form of flowers	3 points
Colour	4 points
Total	**17 points**
Uniformity (for multiple spike classes)	3 points
Total	**20 points**

Floral Arrangements

Fashions in the design of such floral arrangements as baskets, vases, bowls, bouquets and dinner-table decorations change considerably from one period to another, as does the range of flowers and foliage used. Beauty of form and colour, lightness of arrangement, happy harmonies or suitable contrasts always meet with general approval. The use of suitable foliage, berries, fruits and seed pods and accessories may be desirable and permitted or required by the schedule.

The rarity and cost of the flowers should not, as such, influence judges. The schedule will usually convey whether the class is interpretative or a straight-forward arrangement, and may indicate whether the judges should be guided by rules and definitions formulated by the National Association of Flower Arrangement Societies, 21 Denbigh Street, London SW1.

Fuchsias

Meritorious A vigorous, symmetrical, floriferous plant, well furnished with clean foliage and fresh blooms of good colour. Support and ties (if any) neat and unobtrusive. The length of clear stem from the soil to the lowest branch should be as follows: in a standard, not less than 30 in (75 cm); in a half-standard, at least 18 in (45 cm) but less than 30 in (75 cm); in a pyramid, not less than 1 in (2.5 cm).

Defective   A plant that is stunted, ill-balanced or sparsely flowered or that has poor or dirty foliage or has blooms that are not sufficiently open or past their best or that has untidy or obtrusive supports or ties or that has incorrect stem lengths for its group.

Quality and quantity of bloom	. 6	points
Quality and quantity of foliage	. 6	points
Cultural proficiency	. . . 6	points
Presentation	 2	points
Total	. . . . **20**	**points**

Gladioli, Large-flowered

Meritorious   An erect spike, with fresh, unblemished blooms and foliage. A long, well-balanced spike according to cultivar, still carrying the bottom flower and numerous other regularly spaced open and opening flowers and buds, so placed as to hide the stem and gradually narrowing from base to top. An ideal spike would be one third in full flower, one third with buds in colour and one third in green bud. Flowers that are typical of the cultivar and of good form, texture and colour.

Defective   A spike that is bent or has a drooping tip, or carries old or blemished flowers or empty bracts or a spike from which a bract has been removed or one with blemished foliage. A short, ill-balanced or crowded spike or one carrying few open flowers or flowers that are irregularly spaced or so placed that the stem is visible between them. Flowers that are small for the cultivar, of poor form, texture or colour.

Condition	 6	points
Length and form of spike	. . 5	points
Size, form and texture of flowers		
(for the cultivar)	 5	points
Colour	 4	points
Total	. . . . **20**	**points**

Gladioli, Primulinus type

Meritorious   An erect spike, with fresh unblemished blooms and foliage. Stem slender but strong, carrying twelve to twenty flowers and buds. Flowers openly, regularly and gracefully placed, facing forwards with one upper inside petal hooding over the central organs, the whole presenting a light appearance.

Defective A bent or twisted spike, carrying old or blemished flowers or empty bracts. A spike from which a bract has been removed or with blemished foliage. Flowers tightly placed so as to hide the stem, not facing forward and without a hooded upper inside petal. Flowers not typical of the cultivar and heavy in general appearance.

Points As for Large-flowered gladioli (opposite).

Heathers

Meritorious Good condition. Long, straight spikes of evenly spaced florets or large umbels with florets symmetrically arranged. Few unopened buds. No faded florets. Corollas undamaged. Foliage clean, bright-coloured and healthy.

Defective Unsatisfactory condition. Spikes that are short, crooked or uneven, or thinly or irregularly furnished with flowers. Buds not yet open. Florets fading or turning brown. Corollas pierced by insects. Foliage that is dull, withered or unhealthy.

Condition	6 points
Spikes	6 points
Colour	4 points
Uniformity	4 points
Total	**20 points**

Irises, Tall Bearded

Height from 28 in (70 cm) upwards

Meritorious Stems that are sturdy and have at least three branches and that create a shapely and balanced effect. The branches should mostly be of such a length that the flowers, when open, are held away from the stems and from each other.

Well proportioned flowers that are not too large or too small for the height of the stems and have firm substance and breadth in all their petals, both standards and falls. Moderate ruffling of the petals may be an advantage but its absence need not be regarded as a fault. The standards should either stand up firmly or meet so as to give a domed or conical effect. The falls should be flaring or semi-flaring. The colour or combination of colours should be clear but blends of indeterminate colouring may be equally attractive. A slight 'lacing' or serration of the edges of the petals may be an attraction but in excess it is a fault. Fragrance is not of primary importance.

Defective Stems that are weak or have branches that are bunched at the top of the stems or are few in number or are so short that the flowers are held close to the stems or to each other. Flowers that are flimsy in texture or narrow in their petals. Standards that are open or cup-shaped and falls that droop or are tucked under or have unpleasing striation.

Condition, including the number of flowers open at the time of judging	. . . .	. 6 points
Colour	. . . .	. 4 points
Stem and branching	. . .	. 5 points
Quality of standards and falls	.	. 5 points
Total	. . . .	**20 points**

Irises-Intermediate Bearded
Height from 10 to 28 in (25-70 cm)

In general the qualities needed for a good intermediate are the same as those for a good tall bearded iris. It must be realized, however, not only that the stems are shorter but that the flowers are smaller and the branches are fewer in number.

Irises-Dwarf Bearded
Height up to 10 in (25 cm)

Dwarf irises usually have only one or two branches on a stem and only one or two flowers open at a time and the flowers are smaller than the tall and intermediate irises. Apart from these important differences the dwarfs should be judged by the same general rules for quality as those set out for the tall bearded irises.

Irises, Bulbous
(i.e. English, Spanish and Dutch)

Meritorious Stems of full length, strong and upright. Large, fully opened flowers with firm, erect standards and broad, flaring falls. Colours even rather than streaked and flecked (except English irises which seldom have even colouring).

Defective Stems weak or short. Flowers that are small, crowded together or have either weak standards or narrow falls.

Condition	. . . .	. 5 points
Colour	. . . .	. 5 points
Quality and size of flower	.	. 5 points
Stem and foliage	. . . . .	. 5 points
Total	. . . .	**20 points**

Irises, Pacific Coast Section

Judging characteristics for this group of irises are not fully established. The following are suggested, bearing in mind the nature of the plant as grown in the garden. Most are natural or garden hybrids.

Cal-Sibs are hybrids of Pacific Coast and Siberian irises: they should be treated as the former.

Meritorious   Flower stems should be at least 12 in (30 cm) tall (this is necessary for the flowers to stand clear of the foliage), fairly rigid and preferably branched. Flowers should be of clear colours, self or mixed: any markings should be sharp, not smudged. Falls should be broad and nearly overlapping (cf. the corolla of a daffodil), and fully flaring; standards should be upright. The flowers should be well-spaced, not interfering with one another. Two or three flowers per stem would be usual; six or seven would be very exceptional and to be highly commended.

Defective   Narrow falls with large spaces in between. Unclear colours. Falls not uniformly spaced. Stems curling out at the flowers (indicates stems lying flat on ground).

Condition, including the number of flowers open at the time of judging	5 points
Colour	5 points
Stem and branching	5 points
Quality of the falls	5 points
Total	**20 points**

Iris sibirica Section

Meritorious   Stems that are sturdy and have one or more branches. Flowers of good colour that are large and have wide and flaring falls. Lines on the falls that create a pleasing pattern may be an advantage.

Defective   Stems that are weak and have no branching. Flowers that have narrow and very drooping falls.

Condition, including the number of flowers open at the time of judging	5 points
Colour	5 points
Stem and branching	5 points
Quality of the falls	5 points
Total	**20 points**

Orchids

Meritorious A flower of good shape, substance and clear colour or combination of colours, commensurately large for the particular genus or for the specific parents. Numerous flowers in those genera which have more than one flower; not disbudded. Flowers complete, no parts missing. Where shown on a growing plant, as distinct from a cut-flower exhibit, the plant well-grown and not made up of several pieces. A good plant of a species known to be difficult to grow.

Defective Flowers not fully open or damaged, unhealthy or fading. Flowers small for the genus, of poor shape, little substance and of poor colour. A plant that is poorly cultivated, blemished, diseased or otherwise damaged.

Condition	5	points
Flowers: Shape	6	points
Size	6	points
Substance	3	points
Colour	5	points
Difficulty of cultivation	5	points
Total	**30**	**points**

Pansies, Fancy (Exhibition Cultivars)

Meritorious A flower that is large, fresh, clean, circular in outline, with smooth, thick, velvety petals without serrations, lying evenly on each other and either flat or slightly reflexed so that the surface of the flower is slightly convex. Centre petals that meet above the eye and reach well up on the top petals and a bottom petal that is sufficiently deep and broad to balance the others. Colours that are harmonious; belting (margin) of uniform width; blotches that are large, solid, rounded and clearly defined; and an eye that is bright yellow, solid, circular and well defined.

Defective A flower that is less than $2^1/_2$ in (6.3 cm) in diameter, is past its best, soil-marked, concave or lacking a circular outline. Petals that are fish-tailed, thin, of poor substance or serrated. Belting (margin) that is very narrow or more than $^1/_3$ in (84 mm) wide or of uneven width or ill-defined; blotches that are small, thin or ragged-edged; an eye that is dull or ill-defined.

Condition	 3	points
Form and texture	 5	points
Size	 3	points
Colour	 3	points
Belting	 2	points
Blotch	 2	points
Eye	 2	points
Total	. . . . **20**	**points**

Pansies, Show

Meritorious A flower that is from $1^{1}/_{2} - 2$ in (3.8–5 cm) in diameter, fresh and clean and with the same form, build, texture and eye as in a Fancy pansy.

A bicolour flower with a ground-colour of the same shade throughout, circular, broad, of uniform width and well defined at its edge. Belting (margin) of uniform width, of exactly the same colour as the top petals, distinct from the ground-colour and well defined at its junction with the ground-colour. A blotch of good size (though smaller than in a Fancy pansy), dense, solid and approximately circular.

In a 'dark self-coloured' flower: the same shade throughout with no trace of a blotch. In any other 'self-coloured' flower: the same shade throughout except for a blotch as in a bicolour.

Defective A flower that is less than $1^{1}/_{2}$ in (3.8 cm) or over 2 in (5 cm) in diameter, past its best, soil-marked, concave or lacking a circular outline. Petals that are fish-tailed, thin or of poor substance or serrated. Belting (margin) that is very narrow or very wide, of uneven width or ill-defined or not of the same colour as the top petals or not distinct from the ground-colour. Except in a 'dark self-coloured' flower, a blotch that is small, thin or ragged-edged. An eye that is dull or ill-defined.

Points As for Fancy pansies, above

Pelargoniums, Ivy-leaved

Meritorious A floriferous plant of pleasing form. Ample, healthy, clean and bright foliage. Trusses that are fully expanded and clear of the foliage. A bright, clear and decided colour.

Defective A plant that is of unpleasing form or is partly defoliated or has insufficient flowers. Coarse, yellowing, dull or dirty leaves. Trusses that are not fully developed or are not clear of the foliage.

Plant	.8 points
Trusses	.4 points
Pips	.3 points
Colour	.2 points
Foliage	.3 points
Total	**20 points**

Pelargoniums, Zonal and Regal

Meritorious A shapely plant, proportionate to the size of the pot. Trusses should be held well clear of the foliage, proportionate in number to the size of the plant and of bright, clear and distinct colour. Large, round flowers (pips) with broad overlapping petals.

Defective A mis-shapen or partly defoliated plant, with too few trusses for its size. Trusses that are small, thin, or have too few fully expanded flowers (pips) or have weak stems, or stems that do not hold the flowers clear of the foliage. Leaves that are coarse, yellowing or dirty, or that show evidence of insect injury or disease.

Condition	.5 points
Trusses	.5 points
Pips	.3 points
Colour	.4 points
Foliage	.3 points
Total	**20 points**

Pinks

Pinks may be classed according to colour as follows:

Selfs, which must be of one clear colour.

Bi-colours, which must have two colours in concentric zones on every petal; the boundary between the colours should be clear.

Fancies, which may have any ground-colour and be marked or suffused with another contrasting colour or colours on every petal.

Laced Pinks, which may be double, or single with five petals, with laced markings on every petal.

Meritorious Good condition. Flowers that are symmetrical, circular in outline and appear light and dainty. Petals that are of good substance, flat and with edges either smooth or regularly serrated. Guard-petals broad and at right angles to the calyx. In double pinks, inner petals that are evenly disposed, diminishing in size toward the centre. Calyx not split. Stems that are rigid, supporting the flowers so that they face upward or at a slight angle, and carrying subsidiary blooms or buds. Clear, bright, colours and well-defined markings, if any. A strong scent. Glaucous foliage. Uniformity.

Defective Unsatisfactory condition. Flowers that are asymmetrical, not circular in outline, or appearing coarse. Petals that are of poor substance or ribbed. Guard-petals that are narrow or are incurved or recurved. Inner petals of double pinks that are not evenly disposed. Calyx split. Stems not rigid, with flowers that face downward, or that carry no subsidiary blooms or buds. Poor colours or ill-defined markings. Lack of fragrance. Lack of uniformity. Unless specifically permitted by the schedule, exhibits with supports to the stems or calyx-bands should be disqualified.

Form of flower	4 points
Condition	5 points
Colour	3 points
Stem and calyx	4 points
Fragrance	2 points
Uniformity	2 points
Total	**20 points**

Polyanthus

Meritorious Good condition, including healthy, undamaged foliage. Long, stout, erect flower stems. Large, compact, symmetrical trusses. Large, circular, flat pips of good substance. Bright colours.

Defective A plant in poor condition or with unhealthy or damaged foliage. Flower stems that are short, weak or not erect. Trusses that are small or loose or have such short pedicels that the pips overlap unduly. Pips that are small, starry, not flat or of poor substance.

Condition	5 points
Flower-stems	4 points
Trusses	4 points
Pips	4 points
Colour	3 points
Total	**20 points**

Pot Plants and House Plants

*(other than those for which separate criteria are given
elsewhere in this section)*

Pots or containers should be clean and undamaged and where staking, tying or wiring is necessary, it should be neatly done in a manner which does not detract from the appearance of the plant.

Ferns, bromeliads and orchids and similar plants that are naturally epiphytic may be shown attached to a piece of bark or wood instead of in pots and should not be disqualifed in a pot plant class simply because they are not shown with their roots inside a container.

Plants usually grown for their ornamental foliage may not be debarred from foliage plant classes simply because they happen to be in flower at the time of the competition but, if in flower, they must also be considered eligible for entry in flowering plant classes. Judges must consider only the attribute called for in the wording of the class and, if they are judging a foliage class, must take no account of any flowers on a plant, while, when judging a flowering plant class, they must only award points for foliage on the usual scale. For show purposes the highly coloured ornamental bracts on plants such as *Bougainvillea*, *Euphorbia* and *Beloperone (Justicia)* are considered to be an integral part of the flower and do not qualify for consideration as foliage in pot plant classes.

Where it is usual to grow a number of corms, tubers, cuttings or bulbs in a pot to give a well furnished appearance (e.g. *Achimenes*, *Tradescantia* or *Freesia*) the pot is admissible as 'A pot plant' even though there is, strictly speaking, more than one plant in the container.

Flowering or Fruiting Plants

Meritorious   A sturdy, shapely plant, well furnished with healthy, unblemished foliage, displaying flowers, coloured bracts or fruits of good size, colour and substance. Preference should be given to decorative rather than botanical value but, other things being equal, the greater degree of skill required to produce certain plants to perfection should be taken into consideration.

Defective   A drawn, undernourished plant with unhealthy, deformed, undersized, scanty or diseased foliage with undersized flowers, bracts or fruits of poor substance and dull, ill-defined colours. A plant that is easy to grow if in competition with one that is difficult to grow.

Plant	6	points
Quality and quantity of bloom or fruit	6	points
Foliage	4	points
Colour	4	points
Total	**20**	**points**

Foliage Plants (decorative in form and/or colour)

Meritorious A sturdy, shapely plant, well furnished with clean, unblemished, healthy foliage. Though preference should be given to decorative value, all other things being equal, the greater degree of skill required to produce certain plants to perfection should be taken into consideration.

Defective A drawn, undernourished plant with unhealthy, deformed, undersized, scanty or diseased foliage, of little ornamental value. A plant that is easy to grow if in competition with one that is difficult to grow.

Condition	6	points
Decorative value	6	points
Cultivation	5	points
Difficulty of cultivation	3	points
Total	**20**	**points**

Primroses

Meritorious A tufted and compact habit of growth. Foliage that is healthy and undamaged. Numerous flowers, produced singly on long peduncles and forming a symmetrical mass. Flowers of good substance, circular in outline with definite, clear colours.

Defective A plant with a loose habit of growth or with unhealthy or blemished foliage. Flowers that are few or have short stalks or are not arranged symmetrically or are of poor substance or are not circular in outline.

Habit and foliage	2	points
Floriferousness	2	points
Stalk and form of flower	3	points
Colour	3	points
Total	**10**	**points**

Primula malacoides

Meritorious A sturdy, vigorous plant with foliage undamaged and free from blemish and that carries numerous open flowers on graceful, well-balanced trusses. Trusses large with strong but slender stems, carrying the flowers well above the foliage. Flowers well-formed, of good substance and with fresh, clear colours.

Defective A plant that is drawn or weak or has damaged or blemished foliage or few flowers or is ill-balanced. Trusses that are small or lacking in grace. Flowers of poor substance.

Plant	.6 points
Trusses	.5 points
Flowers	.6 points
Colour	.3 points
Total	**20 points**

Primula obconica

Meritorious A vigorous, compact plant with foliage undamaged and free from blemish carrying numerous trusses of open flowers. Trusses that are many-flowered with strong but slender stems carrying the flowers well above the foliage. Flowers that are large with overlapping lobes of good substance and with fresh, clear colours.

Defective A plant that is drawn or weak or has damaged or blemished foliage or has few trusses of flowers for its size. Trusses that are small or have weak stems that do not carry the flowers well above the foliage. Flowers that are small or have narrow lobes or are of poor texture.

Plant	.6 points
Trusses	.5 points
Flowers	.6 points
Colour	.3 points
Total	**20 points**

Primula sinensis (type)

Meritorious A sturdy, vigorous plant with foliage that is undamaged and free from blemish. A large truss, borne on a stout stem above the foliage. Flowers that are large and circular with broad, overlapping lobes of good substance and with fresh, clear colours.

Defective A plant that is drawn or weak or has damaged or blemished foliage. A truss that is small or has a weak stem and does not carry the flowers above the foliage. Flowers that are small or have narrow lobes or are of poor substance.

Plant	6 points
Trusses	5 points
Flowers	6 points
Colour	3 points
Total	**20 points**

Rock-garden Plants.

See Alpine-house and Rock-garden Plants, page 87

Roses

The current classification of roses that has been adopted by the World Federation of Rose Societies is as follows:

Modern Garden Roses: hybrids dating from the introduction of the first Hybrid Tea Rose in 1867 and not including wild or species roses.

Old Garden Roses: cultivars of groups (e.g. Hybrid Perpetuals) already established before 1867.

Wild Roses: species and their hybrids that bear a strong resemblance to species.

The expressions 'Large Flowered' (Hybrid Tea) and 'Cluster Flowered' (Floribunda) apply where appropriate to all types of modern garden roses (Bush / Shrub / Climber / Rambler / Ground Cover / Miniature).

Rose breeding in recent years has tended to blur the distinction between large flowered and cluster flowered blooms to the extent that the breeder is often unsure of the category in which a new rose should be placed. Moreover, the skilled gardener may, by good cultivation and careful disbudding, induce a cultivar normally classed as cluster flowered to produce specimen (large flowered) blooms. Similarly, a cultivar identified as large flowered may be persuaded to produce large clusters of relatively small blooms.

This has resulted in much confusion at exhibitions and the situation is likely only to become worse. As a result it has been decided that the sole criterion for showing roses should be *whether the exhibit meets the requirements of the class in which it is entered. In effect, this means that any type of modern garden rose may be entered in any class without risk of being declared 'not according to schedule'.*

Competitive classes for roses fall into the following four groups:
(1) Classes for specimen blooms of large flowered (HT) roses.

(2)   Classes for large flowered roses, other than specimen blooms and for cluster flowered (Floribunda) roses and all other types of roses grown and staged in clusters.

(3)   Classes for '3 stage blooms'.

(4)   Classes for miniature roses.

Specimen blooms are judged solely on their beauty as individual blooms with or without foliage. They are often shown in boxes but may be displayed singly in specimen vases. Wire supports may be used to keep the blooms erect.

Decorative blooms should, as far as the conditions in the schedule permit, be exhibited in such a way as to show the natural habit of growth and foliage of the cultivar. Any cultivar may be shown (unless otherwise specified in the schedule) and single, semi-double and fully double blooms should be regarded as of equal merit, provided that they are typical in size and other characters of the cultivars.

Roses, Specimen Blooms

Meritorious A bloom that is fresh, free from any blemish, in its most perfect phase and of full size for the cultivar; is of good form with petals of good substance, regularly and gracefully arranged within a circular outline and has a well-formed centre. Colour bright and brilliant. Well-formed foliage of good size and texture, free from blemish due to disease or pests. (Not applicable to box classes).

Defective A bloom that is not fresh or is not in its most perfect phase, is small for the cultivar or so large as to be coarse, is blemished in any way or has petals that are few or thin or has a centre that is split or confused or has obviously been dressed or plucked or is still tied.

Condition and form	3 points
Size and colour	2 points
Total	**5 points**

To the above criteria the following should be added according to the quality of the bloom:

High class blooms	3 points
Medium	2 points
Worthy	1 point

For 'High Class' blooms judged to be superior in quality an optional additional 1 or 2 points may be awarded.

Roses, other than Specimen Blooms

Meritorious Blooms that are fresh, free from any blemish in their most perfect phase, of full size for the cultivar and of the form typical of it. Colour bright and brilliant. Well-formed foliage of good size and texture, free from blemish due to disease or pests. Strong stems proportionate to the blooms.

Defective Blooms that are not fresh or are not in their most perfect phase or are small for the cultivar or so large as to be coarse or are blemished or have thin petals. Foliage that is small, of poor texture or blemished by any disease or pest. Stems that are so weak as to need supports or that are not in proportion to the blooms.

Condition (colour, brilliance and freshness) 6	points
Decorative beauty, form of blooms or truss 6	points
Arrangement 4	points
Stems and foliage 4	points
Total **20**	**points**

3 Stage Large Flowered Roses

Meritorious One bloom in the 'bud' stage, in full colour with one or two petals beginning to unfurl above an opening calyx; one bloom in the 'perfect' stage, half to three quarters open; one bloom in the 'full bloom' stage with the petals symmetrically arranged within a circular outline; the stamens, if exposed, should be fresh and of good colour. Well formed stems and foliage free from distortion or any blemish.

Defective Blooms that are immature or have developed beyond the respective stages, are not typical of the cultivar or that are blemished or of poor colour. Stems weak, bent or damaged, foliage poor, thin or blemished.

Condition (colour, brilliance and freshness) 6	points
Form of blooms 6	points
Arrangement 4	points
Stems and foliage 4	points
Total **20**	**points**

Miniature Roses in Bowls and Vases

Meritorious Roses that are miniature in all aspects of size of flowers, foliage and growth. Blooms may be single, semi-double or double. Blooms fresh, bright in colour, free from blemish and balanced for size and state of development. Stems slim and straight, well furnished with dainty unmarked foliage.

Defective Blooms that are unequal in size or state of development, are not fresh or of bright colour, are not of appropriate size for the variety or are blemished; stems weak or bent; foliage poor, thin, spare or blemished.

Points As for Miniatures in Boxes, see below.

Miniature Roses in Boxes or Similar Containers

Meritorious Blooms all in the same stage of development and equal in size, circular in outline; petals of good substance, brilliant in colour, fresh and free from blemish. Arranged in pleasing colour balance.

Defective Blooms unequal in size and state of development, with poor substance or colour, stale or blemished.

Condition (colour, brilliance and freshness)	. . . . . 6 points
Form	. 6 points
Uniformity	. 4 points
Presentation	. 4 points
Total	**20 points**

For shows organised by The Royal National Rose Society or for rose classes in shows organised by Societies affiliated to the RNRS, the use of the RNRS scale of points may be obligatory. Details of these are contained in the RNRS publication 'Judging Roses' which may be obtained from the Secretary of the RNRS.

Sweet Peas

(Cultivars of Lathyrus odoratus)

Meritorious Strong spikes with well-spaced blooms, the top blooms being well expanded and the bottom blooms still fresh. Large flowers with erect standards and rigid wings, free from colour-running, spotting or scorching and of a bright colour with a silken sheen. Long, straight stems proportionate to the size of the blooms. Effectiveness of staging (particularly when competition is close).

Defective Weak spikes with irregularly placed blooms or having undeveloped or poorly coloured top blooms or with blooms showing seed-pods or losing colour. Flowers small for the cultivar, malformed, spotted or scorched or that have poor or running colour.

Stems crooked or disproportionately short or long for the size of the blooms.

Trueness of colour and freshness of bloom	. . 6	points
Placement of bloom	. . . 5	points
Size and form of bloom	. . 4	points
Stem proportionate to size of bloom	 3	points
Effectiveness of staging	. . . 2	points
Total	. . . . . **20**	**points**

Tulips

Meritorious Flowers in good condition, in their most perfect phase and unblemished, of a good colour for the cultivar, firm substance, smooth texture and of the form typical of the section to which the cultivar belongs. Stems that are stiff and strong enough to carry the flowers without artificial support. Foliage that is stiff.

Defective Flowers that are not fresh or are not in their most perfect phase or are spotted, blistered or otherwise blemished or of poor colour for the cultivar or are thin or of rough texture or not of the form typical of their class. Stems limp or too weak to support the flowers or wired. Foliage limp.

Condition	 4	points
Form	 4	points
Colour	 4	points
Size (for the cultivar)	. . . 2	points
Substance	 3	points
Stems	 3	points
Total	. . . . . **20**	**points**

Violas (Exhibition Cultivars)

Meritorious A flower that is large, fresh, clean and of the form, build and texture outlined for Fancy pansies (see page 110). While the colour may be self, striped, mottled, suffused or belted (margined), there must be no semblance of a blotch or any rays and the eye must be bright, solid, circular and well defined.

Defective A flower that is less than $2^1/_2$ in (6.3 cm) in diameter, past its best, soil-marked, concave or lacking in circular outline. Petals fish-tailed or with V-shaped gaps between them or thin, of poor substance or serrated. Any semblance of a blotch or of rays. An eye that is very large or is square or ill-defined.

Condition	 3	points
Form and texture	 5	points
Size	 3	points
Colour	 7	points
Eye	 2	points
Total	. . . . **20**	**points**

THE JUDGING OF GARDENS AND ALLOTMENTS

The inspection of gardens and allotments in competition with each other should be timed so that a comprehensive assessment of the ornamental or productive value throughout the whole of the year may be made rather than simply judging the entry at its peak. This will normally require the judges to make at least two visits, one in June or the first week in July and another between mid-August and mid-September. Where possible all entries in the competition should be assessed within a maximum period of five days.

The days for judging should be fixed by the competition's organising committee in consultation with the judges, and competitors should be given an indication of when their garden or allotment is likely to be visited.

Competition organisers should ensure that the judge is accompanied by a steward who knows the exact location of all the entrants and has copies of their official entries.

1. The judging of gardens Contemporary domestic gardens fall within three broad categories.

Purely amenity gardens with less than 20% devoted to the production of fruit and/or vegetables.

Dual purpose gardens with between 20 and 50% devoted to the production of fruit and/or vegetables as well as a substantial amenity area.

A utility garden in which more than 50% is devoted to the production of fruit and/or vegetables and only a small space reserved for amenity or ornamental purposes.

In the judging of gardens credit should be given to the best use of the space, the quality of the plants including grassed areas, design and the intelligent placing of plants in suitable locations and aspects.

The overall size of the garden should not be taken into account nor should the diversity or lack of diversity of plants. A limited number of healthy, well grown plants making the best use of the space available is more meritorious than a wide variety of plants poorly grown and overcrowded or sparsely planted. Brown patches in lawns where the spent foliage of spring bulbs such as daffodils or crocuses has recently been mown off must not be considered a demerit. The relative immaturity of some trees or shrubs should not, in itself, be considered a demerit provided that the plant is appropriately sited and, where necessary, properly staked and/or protected.

The following pointing systems are offered as a guide but competition organisers may wish to adapt them to suit their own specific circumstances; where such adaptations are made, the judges should be advised of them when they are invited to judge.

Amenity Gardens

Health, vigour and suitability of plants	100 points
Suitability of design to its site and usage	75 points
Maintenance of paths, structures, lawns and other grassed areas and working areas	50 points
Cultivation and freedom from perennial weeds	50 points
Harmonious blending of colours, shapes and textures	75 points
Total	**350 points**

Dual Purpose Gardens

Health, vigour and suitability of plants in both amenity and kitchen garden areas	100 points
Maintenance of paths, structures, lawns and grassed areas and working areas	50 points
Range and cultivation of plants in the kitchen garden area	75 points
Design and co-ordination of colours, shapes and textures in the amenity area	75 points
Overall integration of the two elements into a single, atractive, practical whole.	50 points
Total	**350 points**

Utility Gardens

Health, vigour, cultivation and arrangement of vegetables, and/or flowers, and/or fruit and/or culinary herb crops	150 points
Planning for regular rotations, and successional plantings to give optimum use of space, year-round produce and to minimise the build-up of pests and soil borne diseases	75 points
Maintenance of paths, crops, supports, cloches, frames and other structures	45 points
Utilisation of boundary walls or fences or other supports for training soft or top fruits or climbing vegetables	45 points

Neatness, practicality, planting and design of
  amenity area and the suitability of its siting
  within the overall garden area   35 points
Total   **350 points**

Alternatively the following pointing system may be used.

Vegetable Gardens

Section 1	Cultivation (cropping scheme, quality of work, cleanliness, stored humus or compost heap).	25 points
Section 2	For potatoes, 12; winter brassicas, 12; onions, 12; carrots, 12; celery, 8; leeks, 8; beetroot, 6; parsnips, 5	75 points
Section 3	For peas, 12; runner or climbing beans, 12; summer brassicas, 12; lettuces, 8; tomatoes, 8; broad beans, 6; dwarf french beans, 6; vegetable marrows, 6	70 points
Section 4	For any other kinds of vegetable not mentioned above (including salads), 3 points each kind; not more than six kinds to receive points in final total.	18 points
	Total	**188 points**

Flower Gardens

Section 1	For general scheme, 30; tasteful arrangement, 20; cultivation and cleanliness, 20	70 points
Section 2	For shrubs and trees, climbers, rock garden, lawn, paths, greenhouse, fences and hedges: 8 each, but only four of these to receive marks	32 points
Section 3	For hardy herbaceous perennials, annuals and biennials, roses, tender plants, window boxes, window plants, etc.: 8 each, but only four of these to receive marks.	32 points
Section 4	For special features	16 points
	Total	**150 points**

Glasshouses, Frames and other Protected Areas

Section 1	Standard of cultivation, 15; utilisation of growing space, 10; cleanliness, 5	30 points
Section 2	Tomatoes, 10; cucumbers, 10; aubergines, 10; peppers, 10; fruit, 10 (only three of these to receive marks)	30 points
Section 3	Ornamental pot plants	20 points
Section 4	Other plants, 5; specialist collections, 15	20 points
	Total	**100 points**

Fruit Gardens

The Garden must contain not less than six kinds of fruits.

Section 1	For the overall planting scheme 12; good pruning, training, tree and bush form and plant supports 12; cultivation, cleanliness, pest and disease control 12	36 points
Section 2	For apples 12, pears 10, plums 10, grapes 10, cherries 8, currants red or white 8, currants black 8, gooseberries 8, raspberries 8, strawberries 8, blackberries or hybrid berries 8	98 points

(The tree and bush fruits to consist of at least 4 plants of any one kind, grapes 1, blackberries and/or hybrid berries 2, strawberries 20 ft (6m) of row and raspberries 20 ft (6m) length of row.)

Section 3	For peach and or nectarine fan trained 10, in bush form 8; fig fan trained 10	28 points
Section 4	For any other kind of fruit not mentioned above 4 points each kind, not more than four kinds to receive points in final total	16 points
	Total	**178 points**

2. The judging of allotments For competition purposes an allotment is considered to be an area of land separate from and in addition to the household garden adjacent to the owner's property; or a plot cultivated by a householder who has no garden as part of his/her own domestic premises.

The primary purpose of an allotment is to provide crops of vegetables, fruit, flowers and culinary herbs for household use and the more completely a plot fulfills this objective the greater should be the credit accorded to it in competition.

Allotments also allow enthusiasts for one particular plant or group of plants to indulge their particular passion and a plot given over to the monoculture of, say, dahlias or carnations must be judged according to the standard and quality of cultivation.

The size of plot should not be a factor for consideration in competition but where there are a great many entries of varying sizes organisers should consider dividing the competition into three or four separate classes according to size.

The following pointing systems are offered as a guide but competition organisers may wish to adapt these to suit local conditions or requirements.

Maximum points

Condition of the plot Plots should be well stocked with crops free from obvious signs of excessive damage by pests, disease or weather. Any unplanted areas where crops have just been harvested or that are about to be planted up should be clean and free from weeds and the soil should be of a good, well cultivated condition and texture. 60

Good workmanship Soil between the crops should contain little or no evidence of weeds. Paths and leisure areas where included should be neatly edged, even and well maintained. Evidence of planting for a constant succession of crops should be given credit. Intelligent use of organic methods of pest control such as the pinching out of broad bean tips to inhibit blackfly or the use of barriers against carrot root fly should be given credit. Supports for those plants that require them should be properly positioned and sturdy enough to withstand bad weather. 50

Quality of crops, flowers, fruit and vegetables and plants All plants should be vigorous, sturdy and free from obvious signs of excessive damage by pests, disease or weather. A broad range of food crops, both vegetables and fruit where the latter is permitted, should be in cultivation and flowers grown for cutting or decoration should be assessed on the same basis as the food crops i.e. with a regard to their health, skill in cultivation and suitability to the site. The inclusion of culinary herbs in the cropping scheme should be considered meritorious. 150

Originality of layout and planting The intelligent adaptation of the layout to suit the needs of the plot-holder, the use of companion planting to reduce damage by pests and a pleasing overall visual effect should be considered meritorious. The cultivation of less common crops and the use of 'no dig' or 'deep bed' methods of cultivation should be given credit. 25

Ingenuity in overcoming local problems
Plot-holders who have overcome difficulties such as oddly shaped sites, difficult soil conditions, exposed aspect or excessive shading and dehydration by an adjacent tree belt should be given credit for raising an acceptable (i.e. usable) standard of crop. 25

Visual aspect of the plot The overall appearance of the plot should be neat and pleasing and the balance of the cultivation, as far as is allowed by local regulations should be as broad as possible. 20

Condition of garden sheds etc. Sheds, if present, should be of a neat and workmanlike appearance both inside and out. Frames, cloches and greenhouses should be clean and well maintained. Pea and bean supports should be sturdy enough for the weight of the crops that they bear and any bird netting should be properly positioned and undamaged so as to afford protection to the crops over which they have been placed. 20

Total   **350**

THE JUDGING OF HANGING BASKETS AND OTHER OUTDOOR PLANTED CONTAINERS

The primary purpose of most hanging baskets, window boxes and tubs is to decorate and improve the appearance of areas or structures which otherwise have little or no plant interest. Alternatively they may extend and complement the planted area of a garden.

Hanging baskets are usually for summer use only but window boxes and tubs may be replanted several times during the year and may contain one or two bold-foliaged semi-permanent shrubs as basic structure planting.

In competition most credit should be given to bright bold colourful displays which succeed in catching the eye without being brash or vulgar.

Plants should be closely grouped and overflow the edges of their container so as to hide or almost hide it. They should be arranged in an attractive, well balanced, symmetrical fashion and must be healthy and well developed with no obvious signs of damage by weather, pests or disease.

The planting should be selected and maintained to ensure an attractive display from early summer to the first autumn frost, unless otherwise specified by the competition schedule.

The flowers and foliage should be harmoniously co-ordinated to blend with each other and their setting. The use of a single colour or one single type of plant e.g. fuchsias or begonias, must not be considered a demerit provided the plants are well grown and attractively presented.

For those who require one, a pointing system is suggested as follows:

Initial impact of colours, and/or textures, and/or scent	50 points
Presentation, balance and symmetry of display	50 points
Quality, health, vigour and appropriateness of planting	70 points
Potential for long-term display	30 points
Total	**200 points**

GLOSSARY

Alpine Loosely applied to any plant that is suitable for a rock garden or alpine house.

Amateur A person who, not being a professional, either personally or with unpaid or paid assistance, maintains a garden or grows plants, flowers, fruit or vegetables for pleasure and enjoyment and not for a livelihood. (It is permissible for an amateur to sell surplus fruit and/or vegetables and/or other horticultural produce, provided that the garden is maintained primarily for the pleasure and enjoyment of the household and not as a means of livelihood.)

Annual A plant that grows from seed and naturally and ordinarily flowers, seeds and dies (irrespective of frost) within twelve months.

Beard The beard-like growth on the falls of some irises. Also a term used to describe the roots of some leeks.

Biennial A plant that grows from seed and ordinarily requires two seasons to complete its life-cycle, growing one year, flowering, seeding and dying in the second.

Bloom 1. The waxy covering of many fruits and vegetables, e.g. of a plum and a grape, and of the leaves and stems of many succulent and other plants. 2. A bloom: one open flower, e.g. of a tulip, or one flower-head, e.g. of a chrysanthemum or dahlia; *(see also Flower head, Spike and Spray)* 3. In bloom: bearing at least one open flower. *(Best Bloom, page 20)*

Bowl A vessel for displaying cut flowers in water or for growing bulbous plants and having a mouth-width measurement at least equal to, but usually greater than, its height. In floral arrangement classes, bowls with one or more than one handle are acceptable.

Bract Usually a small leaf-like structure occurring below the flowers and above the true leaves, but sometimes large and coloured, as in *Euphorbia*.

Bulb An underground modified stem bearing a number of swollen fleshy leaf bases or scale leaves in which food is stored, the whole enclosing the next year's bud, e.g. the bulb of a daffodil, tulip, hyacinth or onion.

Bulbous For horticultural show purposes 'bulbous plants' includes those having bulbs, corms or tubers; 'bulbous' may also refer to a defective attribute such as the swelling of a plant, for example, a leek.

Cactus A plant belonging to the family Cactaceae, e.g. species of *Cereus, Epiphyllum, Mammillaria, Opuntia, Schlumbergera* or Zygocactus.

Calyx The outer set of perianth segments, especially when green.

Challenge A challenge cup or trophy is one that does not become the property of the winner at the first contest but is intended either for periodical (usually annual) contests in perpetuity or to become the property of a competitor only after he/she has won it on a specified number of occasions in accordance with the regulations for the particular cup or trophy.

Class A sub-division of a competitive schedule; one group of comparable exhibits.

Collection An assembly of kinds and/or cultivars (varieties) of plants, flowers, fruits or vegetables in one exhibit.

Conifers Members of the Coniferae, which for show purposes includes the maidenhair tree (*Ginkgo*).

Container A general term, used particularly in connection with floral arrangements, for bowls, vases and other vessels used to display plants or flowers.

Corm For horticultural show purposes, a bulb-like swollen underground stem stored with reserve food, e.g. crocus, cyclamen or gladiolus.

Corolla The inner set of perianth segments, if differing from the outer set, and especially if coloured and showy.

Cultivar The internationally accepted term for what, in English-speaking countries, is commonly known by horticulturists as a 'cultivated variety' or simply a 'variety'. (*See under Variety* for the distinction between a cultivar and a 'botanical variety'.)

Deciduous A deciduous tree or shrub is one having leaves that persist only one season and fall in the autumn.

Dish In horticultural show schedules – a specified number or quantity of a fruit or vegetable constituting one item which may be displayed on a table or on a stand or on a receptacle of any material and of any shape. Unless specially permitted by the schedule, a dish must consist of one cultivar (variety) only.

Display An exhibit in which attractiveness of arrangement and general effect are to be considered of more importance than they would have been had the schedule specified a 'group' or a 'collection'.

Disqualify To remove from the judges' consideration because of non-compliance with the specification in the schedule or with a rule governing the competition.

Entry A notification of an intention to exhibit; a unit submitted for exhibition in a competition or show.

Evergreen A plant that retains its living foliage for at least a full year and is never leafless.

Everlasting A plant with flower heads that retain much of their showy character after being cut and dried.

Falls The three outer segments of an iris flower.

Florets Small individual flowers, especially those in heads, as in a chrysanthemum, dahlia or other members of Compositae.

Flower head For horticultural show purposes, an assemblage of florets grouped together in a single head on a single flower stem, e.g. a disbudded chrysanthemum or a disbudded dahlia.

Foliage 1. The leaves of any plant. 2. Stems bearing only leaves.

Forced Grown to flower or be ready for consumption before the normal time.

Frond A leaf of a fern or palm.

Fruits 1. In classes for edible fruits: 'fruits' means those normally grown for dessert or for eating when cooked as pudding (*see Kind*). 2. In classes for ornamental fruits and for floral arrangements: 'fruits' means all types of developed ovaries, e.g. seed pods, berries and ornamental gourds.

Genus A group of related plants having the same generic name, e.g. all species and hybrids of the genus *Lilium*, such as *Lilium candidum, Lilium chalcedonicum, Lilium* 'Enchantment', *Lilium henryi, Lilium regale* and *Lilium* x *testaceum*.

Grown in the open 1. In classes for fruit the expression means that the plants or trees have flowered and also set their fruit, as well as ripened it, without any protection beyond netting or a wall-coping not exceeding 2 ft (60 cm) in width. 2. In classes for vegetables, for annuals, for plants grown as annuals and for half-hardy ornamental plants, the expression means that the plants have been grown in the ground in the open air without any protection by glass or glass substitute since the danger of spring frosts has passed. 3. In classes for hardy herbaceous plants, trees and shrubs the expression means those grown in the ground in the open air and not with protection by glass or glass substitutes.

Habit The general appearance or manner of growth of a plant e.g. compact, straggling, tufted, bushy, shrubby.

Half-hardy A half-hardy plant is one that may be grown in the open air for part of the year but must be lifted and housed or protected in some other way during the winter. In the case of an annual: one that may either be raised under glass and planted out when frosts are no longer feared or sown out of doors in May or early June.

Hardy A hardy plant is one that is able to survive the average winter when grown in the open without protection.

Herb For horticultural show purposes a culinary 'herb' is a plant possessing some aromatic quality that makes it of value for flavouring soups, stews, sauces, salads, etc., the following being among the more important kinds: angelica, balm, basil, bay, borage, chervil, chives, coriander, dill, fennel, hyssop, lovage, marjoram, mint, parsley, rosemary, sage, savory, sweet cicely (myrrh), tansy, tarragon and thyme. Seed forms such as coriander and dill and root forms such as horseradish should not be included

Herbaceous perennial A plant with a non-woody stem that either dies down to the ground completely each winter, e.g. delphinium, or retains its basal foliage, e.g. bergenia, but which has a rootstock that remains alive throughout several years. For horticultural purposes the word 'rootstock' includes all bulbs, corms, rhizomes and tubers unless specifically excluded by a show schedule.

Herbaceous plant A plant that does not form a persistent woody stem. It may be annual, biennial or perennial.

House plant A plant grown for the decorative effect of its foliage, flower or fruit and which, given reasonable treatment, will thrive in a dwelling room for several years.

Hybrid A plant derived from the interbreeding of two or more genetically distinct plants (in horticulture, usually two or more species), e.g. *Lilium* x *testaceum* is a hybrid resulting from the interbreeding of *Lilium candidum* and *Lilium chalcedonicum;* x *Brassocattleya holfordii* is a hybrid resulting from the interbreeding of *Brassavola digbyana* and *Cattleya forbesii.* F1 hybrids are plants raised from seed obtained from crosses between parents from selected lines.

Inflorescence The flowering portion of the stem above the last stem leaves, including its flower branches, bracts and flowers.

Kind A term recommended for use in the classification of fruit and vegetables for show purposes, e.g. apples, grapes, peaches, pears and plums are 'kinds' of fruit; asparagus, carrots, onions and peas are 'kinds' of vegetable.

While the division of fruit and vegetables into 'kinds' for show purposes is useful and simplifies schedule making there is no real way in which this type of categorisation can be applied to ornamental plants such as annuals, herbaceous plants, trees and shrubs, etc. These plants are all, broadly speaking, either species or cultivars and those with common characteristics are gathered together in groups called genera which in turn are grouped in families. Thus *Iris danfordiae* and the tall bearded *Iris* 'Grace' are a species and a cultivar of the genus *Iris* which in turn is one of the genera of the family Iridaceae. For show purposes, where the object is to attract a wide diversity of plants into a collection class, it is best to word the schedule to invite 'Six hardy herbaceous plants representing at least three genera, one vase of each' or 'Four species or cultivars of bulbous plants representing two or more genera, one vase of each' or similar adaptations of these wordings.

For exhibition purposes the following are different kinds of fruit:

Apples	Loganberries
Apricots	Melons
Blackberries	Medlars
Blueberries	Nectarines
Boysenberries	Oranges
Bullaces	Peaches
Cherries	Plums, including Gages
Currants, Black	Quinces
Currants, Red and White	Raspberries
Damsons	Strawberries
Figs	Sunberries
Filberts and Cobnuts	Tayberries
Gooseberries	Tummelberries
Grapes, Black and White	Walnuts
Lemons	Youngberries

For exhibition purposes the following are different kinds of vegetables:

Artichokes, Chinese	Beans, Dwarf French/Stringless
Artichokes, Globe	
Artichokes, Jerusalem	Beans, Runner and Stringless Runner
Asparagus	
Aubergines	Beetroot
Beans, Broad	Broccoli, Sprouting and Coloured-headed
Beans, Climbing, other than Runner	Brussels Sprouts
	Cabbages, Chinese

Cabbages, Green
Cabbages, Red
Cabbages, Savoy
Carrots
Cauliflowers, including
    White Heading 'Broccoli'
Celeriac
Celery
Chicory
Chives
Corn Salad
Courgettes
Couve Tronchuda
Cress
Cress, American or Land
Cucumbers
Dandelion, Blanched
Endive
Fennel, Florence
Garlic
Kales
Kohl Rabi
Leeks
Lettuces

Marrows, including Squashes
    and other similar edible
    cucurbits
Mushrooms
Mustard or Rape
New Zealand Spinach
Okra
Onions
Parsnips
Peas
Peppers, Sweet and Chili
Potatoes
Pumpkins
Radishes
Rhubarb
Salsify
Scorzonera
Seakale
Seakale Beet
Shallots
Spinach
Spinach Beet
Swedes
Sweet Corn
Tomatoes
Turnips

Leeks For exhibition purposes leeks are divided into three categories:

Pot not more than 6 in (15 cm) from base to button.

Intermediate not less than 6 in (15 cm) and not more than 14 in (35 cm) from base to button.

Blanch more than 14 in (35 cm) from base to button.

Natural 'Natural', as applied to foliage, flowers or fruits, means as produced by the plant, without any artificial treatment such as dyeing, oiling or varnishing.

Novice A competitor who has not won at a previous show some prize or prizes specified in the definition of a novice in the schedule.

Originality In a schedule 'originality' means uncommon or unusual but at the same time desirable.

Panicle For horticultural show purposes, a branched inflorescence.

Pedicel The stalk of a single flower on an inflorescence *(see Peduncle).*

Peduncle The stalk of an inflorescence or of part of an inflorescence. This term should also be used for a stalk of an inflorescence with a solitary flower. *(See also Pedicel.)*

Perennial A perennial plant is one that lives for more than two years. Perennial plants include trees and shrubs, plants that grow from bulbs, corms, rhizomes and tubers and, in fact, all that are not annuals or biennials. (Antirrhinums, petunias, wallflowers and some other plants are usually grown as annuals or biennials in gardens but, botanically, may be true perennials. In such cases, it is recommended that the horticultural practice of treating them as annuals should be adopted for show purposes to avoid confusion.) *See page 26, paragraph 17.*

Perianth A term used for the calyx and corolla or their equivalents but seldom used except when the segments of the two whorls are both coloured, as in a daffodil or a tulip.

Petal An individual segment of the corolla, especially one free to the base.

Pip 1. An individual flower of an inflorescence, applied especially to auriculas, delphiniums, gladioli and sweet williams. 2. A bulbil within the inflorescence of leeks, onions and other alliums. 3. The seed within a fruit such as apple, strawberry, etc.

Pot plant For horticultural show purposes, a plant grown in a pot for the decorative effect of its foliage, flower or fruit and for use in a glasshouse or, for a short period, in a dwelling room.

Professional A person who gains his/her livelihood by growing horticultural plants, flowers, fruit or vegetables for sale or for an employer or anyone employed in the maintenance of a garden, pleasure ground or park.

Ray-florets The outer florets of a flower head, such as that of a daisy, often larger than the inner florets.

Rhizome An underground, usually horizontal, swollen stem containing food reserves, e.g. bearded irises.

Rootstock or stock In the context of fruit refers to the plant on to which the fruit-bearing material has been grafted or budded. It can also applies to the stocks used in the grafting or budding of ornamental plants.

Root vegetable For horticultural show purposes, root vegetables include the following kinds: artichokes (Chinese and Jerusalem), beetroot, carrots, celeriac, kohl rabi, parsnips, potatoes, radishes, salsify, scorzonera, swedes and turnips.

Salading or salad vegetable A vegetable used in either a raw or cooked state and served in salads as a cold dish. The following kinds may be used for horticultural show purposes: beetroot, cabbages, carrots, celeriac, celery, chicory, chives, corn salad or lambs' lettuce, cress, cress (American or land), cucumbers, dandelion (blanched), endive, florence fennel, kohl rabi, lettuces, mustard or rape, onions (green salad), potatoes, radishes, sweet peppers, tomatoes, turnips and watercress.

Scape A long, naked or nearly naked peduncle, whether one- or many-flowered, rising directly from the base of a plant.

Seedling 1. A young plant that has recently germinated. 2. A plant of any age raised from seed as opposed to one propagated by grafting or other vegetative means. 3. For horticultural purposes a distinct new cultivar (variety) raised from seed and not yet named.

Sepal An individual segment of the calyx.

Shrub A woody perennial, often many-stemmed, of smaller structure than a tree and having no distinct bole or trunk.

Soft fruit A fruit having a soft texture and numerous seeds, e.g. a blackberry, currant, gooseberry, loganberry, raspberry or strawberry.

Species A group of closely related plants of one genus having the same specific name; e.g. *Lilium candidum, Lilium henryi, Lilium martagon* and *Lilium regale* are four species of *Lilium; Lilium martagon* var. *cattaniæ* and *Lilium martagon* var. *hirsutum* are both botanical varieties of one species, *Lilium martagon.*

Spike For horticultural show purposes a spike is an unbranched (or only very slightly branched) inflorescence with an elongated axis, bearing either stalked or stalkless flowers, as in a cymbidium, delphinium, foxglove, gladiolus, hollyhock or odontoglossum.

Sport A sport from a particular cultivar (variety) is a plant propagated vegetatively from a mutated part of the parent cultivar (variety).

Spray For horticultural show purposes, a spray is a branched, many-flowered inflorescence usually on a single main stem.

Standard 1. A term which, when applied to a tree or other plant, means a specimen with an upright stem of some length supporting a head, e.g. the standard is a common form for 'permanent' orchard trees of apples, pears and plums. Roses, fuchsias, heliotropes and chrysanthemums are some ornamental plants readily grown as standards. 2. When applied to a sweet pea or other papilionaceous flowers it describes the, usually upright, back petal of the corolla. 3. When applied to an iris it describes one of the three inner perianth segments.

Stone fruit A fruit with a soft, fleshy interior, surrounding a comparatively large 'stone' containing, usually, a solitary seed, e.g. an apricot, cherry, damson, peach or plum.

Strig A term relating to currants and to berries of a similar bearing habit such as Jostaberry and Worcesterberry. Strig indicates a bunch or, in botanical terms, a complete raceme or panicle of berries. It is best detached from the plant with scissors and should not include any of the woody section at the base.

Succulent A plant with very fleshy leaves or stems or both, e.g. species of *Bryophyllum, Cotyledon, Crassula, Echeveria, Hoya, Kalanchoe, Sedum, Sempervivum* and most Cactaceae.

Tender A tender plant is one that requires a favourable locality or situation and that, under severe climatic conditions, may need some form of protection during the winter.

Tree A perennial woody plant with an evident bole or trunk, but sometimes multi-stemmed.

Truss A cluster of flowers or fruits growing from one main stem, as in a pelargonium, polyanthus, rhododendron or tomato.

Tuber A swollen underground stem with buds or 'eyes' from which new plants or tubers are produced, e.g. Jerusalem artichoke, tuberous begonia, dahlia, gloriosa, gloxinia, potato and runner beans.

Uniformity The state of being alike in size, shape and colour.

Variety In scientific usage the term 'variety' (*varietas*) is a botanical category restricted to a naturally occurring variant of a species; 'botanical varieties' are given Latin names, preceded by the abbreviation var. and begin with a small letter (e.g. *Paeonia lutea* var. *ludlowii*). Variants of species and hybrids produced by man in cultivation are termed cultivars and are given non-Latin 'fancy' names, though some old cultivars, which have had Latin names for many years, retain these names; cultivar names begin with a capital letter and follow directly after the Latin or English name of the species or hybrid concerned, enclosed in single quotation marks (e.g. *Syringa vulgaris* 'Mont Blanc'; Rose 'Peace'; *Juniperus procumbens* 'Nana'; *Viburnum* x *bodnantense* 'Dawn'). In English-speaking countries horticulturists have long used the word 'variety' to cover both 'botanical variety' and 'cultivar', but as the term 'cultivar' is now becoming increasingly accepted, it is recommended that it should be used in show schedules when appropriate.

Vase A vessel for displaying cut flowers in water and having a greater height than the width-measurement of its mouth. Unless otherwise required or permitted by the schedule a vase may contain only one cultivar (variety). In floral arrangement classes, vases with one or more than one handle are acceptable. Where standard vases are not provided by show organisers, judges should exercise discretion in regarding as eligible any container which fulfils the function of a vase and conforms to the definition given above, provided that no account is taken of the container when judging the material shown in it.

Vegetable For horticultural show purposes, a vegetable is a plant (or part of a plant) normally grown in the kitchen garden to be eaten either cooked or less often raw but not usually as dessert or as a pudding. Rhubarb, though commonly eaten as pudding, is classified as a vegetable. Tomatoes, sweet peppers and aubergines, though botanically fruits, are here classified as vegetables.

CLASSIFIED LIST OF FRUITS

For exhibition purposes it is necessary to distinguish between dessert and cooking cultivars and the following lists are drawn up for this purpose alone. Apples, pears and plums must be exhibited as dessert or cooking cultivars in accordance with these lists. Asterisks (*) indicate russet cultivars of dessert apples.

Apples, Dessert

Adams's Pearmain
Allen's Everlasting*
Allington Pippin
American Mother
Ard Cairn Russet*
Aromatic Russet*
Ashmead's Kernel*
Ashmead's Kernel Improved*
Autumn Pearmain
Baker's Delicious
Barnack Beauty
Barnack Orange
Baumann's Reinette
Beauty of Bath
Beauty of Bedford
Beauty of Blackmoor
Beauty of Hants
Belle de Boskoop, small fruits
Ben's Red
Bess Pool
Blenheim Orange, small fruits
Bolero
Boston Russet*
Braddick's Nonpareil
Brownlee's Russet*
Calville Blanc d'Hiver
Captain Kidd
Charles Ross, small fruits
Cherry Cox
Chivers' Delight
Christmas Pearmain
Claygate Pearmain
Cockle's Pippin*
Colonel Vaughan (Kentish Pippin)

Cornish Aromatic
Cornish Gilliflower
Coronation
Court Pendu Plat
Cox's Orange Pippin
Crimson Cox's Orange Pippin
Crispin (Mutsu), small fruits
Crowngold
Cutler Grieve
D'Arcy Spice*
Delicious
Devonshire Quarrenden
Discovery
Duchess's Favourite
Duke of Devonshire*
Easter Orange
Egremont Russet*
Ellison's Orange
Elstar
Exeter Cross
Fearn's Pippin
Feltham Beauty
Fiesta
Gala
Gascoyne's Scarlet, small fruits
Gavin
George Carpenter
George Cave
Gladstone
Gloster 69
Golden Delicious
Golden Reinette
Golden Russet*
Goldilocks
Granny Smith

Gravenstein
Greensleeves
Herring's Pippin, small fruits
Heusgen's Golden Reinette
High View Pippin
Hitchin Pippin
Holstein
Houblon
Hubbard's Pearmain
Idared
Ingrid Marie
Irish Peach
James Grieve
Jerseymac
Jester
Joaneting (white)
John Standish
Jonagold
Jonagored
Jonathan
Joy Bells
Jupiter
Katy (Katja)
Kent
Kerry Pippin
Kidd's Orange Red
King George V
King of the Pippins
King of Tompkins County
King's Acre Pippin
Lady Sudeley
Langley Pippin
Laxton's Advance
Laxton's Early Crimson
Laxton's Epicure
Laxton's Exquisite
Laxton's Fortune
Laxton's Herald
Laxton's Pearmain
Laxton's Superb
Laxton's Victory
Lord Burghley
Lord Hindlip
Lord Lambourne
Mabbott's Pearmain

McIntosh Red
Madresfield Court
Maidstone Favourite
Mannington's Pearmain
Margaret, or Red Joneating
Margil
May Queen
Melba
Merton Beauty
Merton Charm
Merton Joy
Merton Knave
Merton Prolific
Merton Russet*
Merton Worcester
Miller's Seeding
Millicent Barnes
Nanny
Newtown Pippin
Nonpareil *
Norfolk Royal
Norfolk Royal Russet *
Northern Spy
Nutmeg Pippin*
Orleans Reinette
Owen Thomas
Paroquet
Pearl
Pine Golden Pippin*
Pineapple Russet*
Pitmaston Nonpareil*
  (Pitmaston Russet*)
Pitmaston Pine Apple*
Pixie
Polka
Red Astrachan
Red Delicious
Red Ellison
Red Melba
Redsleeves
Reinette du Canada*
Reinette Rouge Etoilée
  (Calville Rouge Précoce)
Renown
Ribston Pippin

Rival
Rosemary Russet*
Ross Nonpareil
Roundway Magnum Bonum,
  small fruits
Royal Gala (Tenroy)
Rubinette
Rushock Pearmain*
St Cecilia
St Edmund's Pippin*,
  (St Edmund's Russet*)
St Everard
Saltcote Pippin
Sanspareil
Scarlet Nonpareil
Siddington Russet*
Sir John Thornycroft
Spartan
Stark's Earliest
Sturmer Pippin
Summerred
Sunset

Suntan
Syke House Russet*
Tydeman's Early Worcester
Tydeman's Late Orange
Vistabella
Wagener
Waltz
Wealthy
Werder Golden Reinette
Wheeler's Russet*
White Astrachan
White Nonpareil
White Transparent
William Crump
William's Favourite
Winston
Winter Quoining (Queening)
Woolbrook Pippin
Worcester Pearmain
Wyken Pippin*
Yellow Ingestrie

Apples, Cooking

A.W. Barnes
Alfriston
Annie Elizabeth
Arthur Turner
Baron Wolseley (Dewdney's)
Beauty of Kent
Beauty of Stoke
Belle de Boskoop, large fruits
Bismarck
Blenheim Orange, large fruits
Bountiful
Bow Hill Pippin
Bramley's Seedling
Broad Eyed Pippin
Bushey Grove
Byford Wonder
Catshead
Cellini
Charles Eyre
Charles Ross, large fruits
Chelmsford Wonder

Cottenham Seedling
Cox's Pomona
Crawley Beauty
Crimson Bramley's Seedling
Crimson Peasgood's Nonsuch
Crispin (Mutsu), large fruits
Domino
Duchess of Oldenburg
Dumelow's Seedling
  (Wellington or Normanton
  Wonder)
Eady's Magnum
Ecklinville
Edward VII
Emneth Early, (Early Victoria)
Emperor Alexander
Encore
French Crab
Galloway Pippin
Gascoyne's Scarlet, large fruits
George Neal

Gloria Mundi
Gold Medal
Golden Noble
Golden Spire
Gooseberry
Grange's Pearmain
Grenadier
Hambledon Deux Ans
Hambling's Seedling
Harvey
Hawthornden
Herring's Pippin, large fruits
Hoary Morning
Hollandbury
Hormead Pearmain
Howgate Wonder
John Waterer
Kentish Fillbasket
Keswick Codlin
King's Acre Bountiful
Lady Henniker
Lane's Prince Albert
Lemon Pippin
Lodi
Lord Derby
Lord Grosvenor
Lord Stradbroke
Lord Suffield
Mère de Ménage
Monarch
Mrs Barron
Nancy Jackson
New Bess Poole
New Hawthornden
New Northern Greening
Newton Wonder
Norfolk Beauty

Norfolk Beefing
Northern Greening
Ontario
Peasgood's Nonsuch
Pott's Seedling
Queen
Queen Caroline (Spencer's Favourite)
Red Victoria
Rev. W. Wilks
Rhode Island Greening
Roundway Magnum Bonum, large fruits
Royal Jubilee
Royal Late Cooking
Royal Russet
Sandringham
Schoolmaster
Shoesmith
Sowman's Seedling
Stirling Castle
Stone's (Loddington)
Striped Beefing
S.T.Wright
Tom Putt
Thomas Rivers
Tower of Glamis
Twenty Ounce
Upton Pyne
Wadhurst Pippin
Waltham Abbey Seedling
Warner's King
Washington
Woolbrook Russet
Yorkshire Beauty
Yorkshire Greening

Bullaces

All bullaces rank as cooking fruits.

Damsons

All damsons rank as cooking fruits.

Pears

The following are classified as cooking pears at RHS Shows:

Belle des Arbres
Bellisme d'Hiver
Beurré Clairgeau
Black Worcester
Catillac
Directeur Alphand
Double de Guerre
Duchesse de Mouchy
General Todleben
Gilogil
Grosse Calebasse
Idaho
King Edward
Old Warden
Ramilies
Summer Compôte
Uvedale's St Germain
Verulam
Vicar of Winkfield
Winter Bon Chrétien
Winter Orange

Plums, Dessert

Allgrove's Superb
Angelina Burdett
Anna Spath
Ariel
Avalon
Bonne de Bry
Coe's Golden Drop
Coe's Violet
Crimson Drop
Decaisne
Denniston's Superb
Excalibur
Gages, all cultivars
Golden Esperen
Goldfinch
Kirke's
Laxton's Delicious
Laxton's Delight
Merton Gem
Ontario
Opal
Orpington Prolific
Oullins Golden
Prince of Wales
Reeves Seedling
Sanctus Hubertus
Severn Cross
Thames Cross
Utility
Victoria
Washington

Plums, Cooking

Admiral
Archduke
Automne Compôte
Belgian Purple
Belle de Louvain
Belle de Septembre
Blackbird
Blaisdon Red
Blue Rock
Boulouf
Cox's Emperor
Curlew
Czar
Diamond
Early Laxton
Early Prolific (Early Rivers)
Edwards
Evesham Wonder
Giant Prune
Gisborne's
Goliath
Heron

Late Orange
Late Rivers
Laxton's Bountiful
Laxton's Cropper
Magnum Bonum,
 Red and White
Marjorie's Seedling
Martin's Seedling
Mirabelle
Monarch
Myrobalan

Orleans, all cultivars
Pershore
Pond's Seedling
President
Primate
Prince Englebert
Purple Pershore
Sultan
Warwickshire Drooper
Winesour
Wyedale

INDEX